ZHOU ENLAI

ZHOU ENLAI

Dorothy and Thomas Hoobler

CHELSEA HOUSE PUBLISHERS
NEW YORK
PHILADELPHIA

SENIOR EDITOR: William P. Hansen
PROJECT EDITOR: John W. Selfridge
ASSOCIATE EDITOR: Marian W. Taylor
EDITORIAL COORDINATOR: Karyn Gullen Browne
EDITORIAL STAFF: Pierre Hauser
Perry Scott King
Kathleen McDermott
Howard Ratner
Alma Rodriguez-Sokol
Bert Yaeger
ART DIRECTOR: Susan Lusk
LAYOUT: Irene Friedman
ART ASSISTANTS: Noreen Lamb
Victoria Tomaselli
COVER ILLUSTRATION: Michael Garland
PICTURE RESEARCH: Matt Miller

3 5 7 9 8 6 4 2

Library of Congress Cataloging in Publication Data

Hoobler, Dorothy, and Hoobler, Thomas. ZHOU ENLAI

(World leaders past & present)
Bibliography: p.
Includes index
1. Chou, En-lai, 1898–1976. 2. Prime ministers—
China—Biography. I. Hoobler, Thomas. II. Title.
III. Series.
DS778.C593H66 1986   951.05′092′4 [B]   85-26926

ISBN 0-87754-516-2

0-7910-0607-7 (pbk.)

China – Politics + Gov't – Biography

Photos courtesy of AP/Wide World Photos, Art Resource, Bettmann Archive,
the Chinese Mission to the United Nations, Culver Pictures, Eastfoto, New
China Pictures Company, Pictorial Parade, UPI/Bettman Newsphotos

Contents

JOHN ADAMS
JOHN QUINCY ADAMS
KONRAD ADENAUER
ALEXANDER THE GREAT
SALVADOR ALLENDE
MARC ANTONY
CORAZON AQUINO
YASIR ARAFAT
KING ARTHUR
HAFEZ AL-ASSAD
KEMAL ATATÜRK
ATTILA
CLEMENT ATTLEE
AUGUSTUS CAESAR
MENACHEM BEGIN
DAVID BEN-GURION
OTTO VON BISMARCK
LÉON BLUM
SIMON BOLÍVAR
CESARE BORGIA
WILLY BRANDT
LEONID BREZHNEV
JULIUS CAESAR
JOHN CALVIN
JIMMY CARTER
FIDEL CASTRO
CATHERINE THE GREAT
CHARLEMAGNE
CHIANG KAI-SHEK
WINSTON CHURCHILL
GEORGES CLEMENCEAU
CLEOPATRA
CONSTANTINE THE GREAT
HERNÁN CORTÉS
OLIVER CROMWELL
GEORGES-JACQUES
   DANTON
JEFFERSON DAVIS
MOSHE DAYAN
CHARLES DE GAULLE
EAMON DE VALERA
EUGENE DEBS
DENG XIAOPING
BENJAMIN DISRAELI
ALEXANDER DUBČEK
FRANÇOIS & JEAN-CLAUDE
   DUVALIER
DWIGHT EISENHOWER
ELEANOR OF AQUITAINE
ELIZABETH I
FAISAL
FERDINAND & ISABELLA
FRANCISCO FRANCO
BENJAMIN FRANKLIN

FREDERICK THE GREAT
INDIRA GANDHI
MOHANDAS GANDHI
GIUSEPPE GARIBALDI
AMIN & BASHIR GEMAYEL
GENGHIS KHAN
WILLIAM GLADSTONE
MIKHAIL GORBACHEV
ULYSSES S. GRANT
ERNESTO "CHE" GUEVARA
TENZIN GYATSO
ALEXANDER HAMILTON
DAG HAMMARSKJÖLD
HENRY VIII
HENRY OF NAVARRE
PAUL VON HINDENBURG
HIROHITO
ADOLF HITLER
HO CHI MINH
KING HUSSEIN
IVAN THE TERRIBLE
ANDREW JACKSON
JAMES I
WOJCIECH JARUZELSKI
THOMAS JEFFERSON
JOAN OF ARC
POPE JOHN XXIII
POPE JOHN PAUL II
LYNDON JOHNSON
BENITO JUÁREZ
JOHN KENNEDY
ROBERT KENNEDY
JOMO KENYATTA
AYATOLLAH KHOMEINI
NIKITA KHRUSHCHEV
KIM IL SUNG
MARTIN LUTHER KING, JR.
HENRY KISSINGER
KUBLAI KHAN
LAFAYETTE
ROBERT E. LEE
VLADIMIR LENIN
ABRAHAM LINCOLN
DAVID LLOYD GEORGE
LOUIS XIV
MARTIN LUTHER
JUDAS MACCABEUS
JAMES MADISON
NELSON & WINNIE
   MANDELA
MAO ZEDONG
FERDINAND MARCOS
GEORGE MARSHALL

MARY, QUEEN OF SCOTS
TOMÁŠ MASARYK
GOLDA MEIR
KLEMENS VON METTERNICH
JAMES MONROE
HOSNI MUBARAK
ROBERT MUGABE
BENITO MUSSOLINI
NAPOLÉON BONAPARTE
GAMAL ABDEL NASSER
JAWAHARLAL NEHRU
NERO
NICHOLAS II
RICHARD NIXON
KWAME NKRUMAH
DANIEL ORTEGA
MOHAMMED REZA PAHLAVI
THOMAS PAINE
CHARLES STEWART
   PARNELL
PERICLES
JUAN PERÓN
PETER THE GREAT
POL POT
MUAMMAR EL-QADDAFI
RONALD REAGAN
CARDINAL RICHELIEU
MAXIMILIEN ROBESPIERRE
ELEANOR ROOSEVELT
FRANKLIN ROOSEVELT
THEODORE ROOSEVELT
ANWAR SADAT
HAILE SELASSIE
PRINCE SIHANOUK
JAN SMUTS
JOSEPH STALIN
SUKARNO
SUN YAT-SEN
TAMERLANE
MOTHER TERESA
MARGARET THATCHER
JOSIP BROZ TITO
TOUSSAINT L'OUVERTURE
LEON TROTSKY
PIERRE TRUDEAU
HARRY TRUMAN
QUEEN VICTORIA
LECH WALESA
GEORGE WASHINGTON
CHAIM WEIZMANN
WOODROW WILSON
XERXES
EMILIANO ZAPATA
ZHOU ENLAI

CHELSEA HOUSE PUBLISHERS

ON LEADERSHIP
Arthur M. Schlesinger, jr.

LEADERSHIP, it may be said, is really what makes the world go round. Love no doubt smooths the passage; but love is a private transaction between consenting adults. Leadership is a public transaction with history. The idea of leadership affirms the capacity of individuals to move, inspire and mobilize masses of people so that they act together in pursuit of an end. Sometimes leadership serves good purposes, sometimes bad; but whether the end is benign or evil, great leaders are those men and women who leave their personal stamp on history.

Now, the very concept of leadership implies the proposition that individuals can make a difference. This proposition has never been universally accepted. From classical times to the present day, eminent thinkers have regarded individuals as no more than the agents and pawns of larger forces, whether the gods and goddesses of the ancient world or, in the modern era, race, class, nation, the dialectic, the will of the people, the spirit of the times, history itself. Against such forces, the individual dwindles into insignificance.

So contends the thesis of historical determinism. Tolstoy's great novel *War and Peace* offers a famous statement of the case. Why, Tolstoy asked, did millions of men in the Napoleonic wars, denying their human feelings and their common sense, move back and forth across Europe slaughtering their fellows? "The war," Tolstoy answered, "was bound to happen simply because it was bound to happen." All prior history predetermined it. As for leaders, they, Tolstoy said, "are but the labels that serve to give a name to an end and, like labels, they have the least possible connection with the event." The greater the leader, "the more conspicuous the inevitability and the predestination of every act he commits." The leader, said Tolstoy, is "the slave of history."

Determinism takes many forms. Marxism is the determinism of class, Nazism the determinism of race. But the idea of men and women as the slaves of history runs athwart the deepest human instincts. Rigid determinism abolishes the idea of human freedom—the assumption of free choice that underlies every move we make, every word we speak, every thought we think. It abolishes the idea of human responsibility, since it is manifestly unfair to reward or punish people for actions that are by definition beyond their control. No one can live consistently by any deterministic creed. The Marxist states prove this themselves by their extreme susceptibility to the cult of leadership.

More than that, history refutes the idea that individuals make no difference. In December 1931 a British politician crossing Park Avenue in New York City between 76th and 77th Streets around ten-thirty at night looked in the wrong direction and was knocked down by an automobile—a moment, he later recalled, of a man aghast, a world aglare: "I do not understand why I was not broken like an eggshell or squashed like a gooseberry." Fourteen months later an American politician, sitting in an open car in Miami, Florida, was fired on by an assassin; the man beside him was hit. Those who believe that individuals make no difference to history might well ponder whether the next two decades would have been the same had Mario Contasini's car killed Winston Churchill in 1931 and Giuseppe Zangara's bullet killed Franklin Roosevelt in 1933. Suppose, in addition, that Adolf Hitler had been killed in the street fighting during the Munich *Putsch* of 1923 and that Lenin had died of typhus during the First World War. What would the 20th century be like now?

For better or for worse, individuals do make a difference. "The notion that a people can run itself and its affairs anonymously," wrote the philosopher William James, "is now well known to be the silliest of absurdities. Mankind does nothing save through initiatives on the part of inventors, great or small, and imitation by the rest of us—these are the sole factors in human progress. Individuals of genius show the way, and set the patterns, which common people then adopt and follow."

Leadership, James suggests, means leadership in thought as well as in action. In the long run, leaders in thought may well make the greater difference to the world. But, as Woodrow Wilson once said, "Those only are leaders of men, in the general eye, who lead in action. . . . It is at their hands that new thought gets its translation into the crude language of deeds." Leaders in thought often invent in solitude and obscurity, leaving to later generations the tasks of imitation. Leaders in action—the leaders portrayed in this series—have to be effective in their own time.

And they cannot be effective by themselves. They must act in response to the rhythms of their age. Their genius must be adapted, in a phrase of William James's, "to the receptivities of the moment." Leaders are useless without followers. "There goes the mob," said the French politician hearing a clamor in the streets. "I am their leader. I must follow them." Great leaders turn the inchoate emotions of the mob to purposes of their own. They seize on the opportunities of their time, the hopes, fears, frustrations, crises, potentialities.

They succeed when events have prepared the way for them, when the community is waiting to be aroused, when they can provide the clarifying and organizing ideas. Leadership ignites the circuit between the individual and the mass and thereby alters history.

It may alter history for better or for worse. Leaders have been responsible for the most extravagant follies and most monstrous crimes that have beset suffering humanity. They have also been vital in such gains as humanity has made in individual freedom, religious and racial tolerance, social justice and respect for human rights.

There is no sure way to tell in advance who is going to lead for good and who for evil. But a glance at the gallery of men and women in *World Leaders—Past and Present* suggests some useful tests.

One test is this: do leaders lead by force or by persuasion? By command or by consent? Through most of history leadership was exercised by the divine right of authority. The duty of followers was to defer and to obey. "Theirs not to reason why,/ Theirs but to do and die." On occasion, as with the so-called "enlightened despots" of the 18th century in Europe, absolutist leadership was animated by humane purposes. More often, absolutism nourished the passion for domination, land, gold and conquest and resulted in tyranny.

The great revolution of modern times has been the revolution of equality. The idea that all people should be equal in their legal condition has undermined the old structures of authority, hierarchy and deference. The revolution of equality has had two contrary effects on the nature of leadership. For equality, as Alexis de Tocqueville pointed out in his great study *Democracy in America*, might mean equality in servitude as well as equality in freedom.

"I know of only two methods of establishing equality in the political world," Tocqueville wrote. "Rights must be given to every citizen, or none at all to anyone . . . save one, who is the master of all." There was no middle ground "between the sovereignty of all and the absolute power of one man." In his astonishing prediction of 20th-century totalitarian dictatorship, Tocqueville explained how the revolution of equality could lead to the "*Führerprinzip*" and more terrible absolutism than the world had ever known.

But when rights are given to every citizen and the sovereignty of all is established, the problem of leadership takes a new form, becomes more exacting than ever before. It is easy to issue commands and enforce them by the rope and the stake, the concentration camp and the *gulag*. It is much harder to use argument and achievement to overcome opposition and win consent. The Founding Fathers of the United States understood the difficulty. They believed that history had given them the opportunity to decide, as

Alexander Hamilton wrote in the first Federalist Paper, whether men are indeed capable of basing government on "reflection and choice, or whether they are forever destined to depend . . . on accident and force."

Government by reflection and choice called for a new style of leadership and a new quality of followership. It required leaders to be responsive to popular concerns, and it required followers to be active and informed participants in the process. Democracy does not eliminate emotion from politics; sometimes it fosters demagoguery; but it is confident that, as the greatest of democratic leaders put it, you cannot fool all of the people all of the time. It measures leadership by results and retires those who overreach or falter or fail.

It is true that in the long run despots are measured by results too. But they can postpone the day of judgment, sometimes indefinitely, and in the meantime they can do infinite harm. It is also true that democracy is no guarantee of virtue and intelligence in government, for the voice of the people is not necessarily the voice of God. But democracy, by assuring the rights of opposition, offers built-in resistance to the evils inherent in absolutism. As the theologian Reinhold Niebuhr summed it up, "Man's capacity for justice makes democracy possible, but man's inclination to injustice makes democracy necessary."

A second test for leadership is the end for which power is sought. When leaders have as their goal the supremacy of a master race or the promotion of totalitarian revolution or the acquisition and exploitation of colonies or the protection of greed and privilege or the preservation of personal power, it is likely that their leadership will do little to advance the cause of humanity. When their goal is the abolition of slavery, the liberation of women, the enlargement of opportunity for the poor and powerless, the extension of equal rights to racial minorities, the defense of the freedoms of expression and opposition, it is likely that their leadership will increase the sum of human liberty and welfare.

Leaders have done great harm to the world. They have also conferred great benefits. You will find both sorts in this series. Even "good" leaders must be regarded with a certain wariness. Leaders are not demigods; they put on their trousers one leg after another just like ordinary mortals. No leader is infallible, and every leader needs to be reminded of this at regular intervals. Irreverence irritates leaders but is their salvation. Unquestioning submission corrupts leaders and demeans followers. Making a cult of a leader is always a mistake. Fortunately hero worship generates its own antidote. "Every hero," said Emerson, "becomes a bore at last."

The signal benefit the great leaders confer is to embolden the rest of us to live according to our own best selves, to be active, insistent, and resolute in affirming our own sense of things. For great leaders attest to the reality of human freedom against the supposed inevitabilities of history. And they attest to the wisdom and power that may lie within the most unlikely of us, which is why Abraham Lincoln remains the supreme example of great leadership. A great leader, said Emerson, exhibits new possibilities to all humanity. "We feed on genius. . . . Great men exist that there may be greater men."

Great leaders, in short, justify themselves by emancipating and empowering their followers. So humanity struggles to master its destiny, remembering with Alexis de Tocqueville: "It is true that around every man a fatal circle is traced beyond which he cannot pass; but within the wide verge of that circle he is powerful and free; as it is with man, so with communities."

—New York

1

The Little Southerner

We should study for China to arise.
—ZHOU ENLAI
as a student at
Nankai Middle School

In 1927 China was a nation in turmoil. Fifteen years earlier, the last imperial dynasty had been overthrown. The Chinese government that took its place had not been powerful enough to rule effectively. In the years that followed, local warlords raised armies that took control of portions of the huge country.

Among those trying to reestablish a national, republican government was Zhou Enlai, a young man of 29 who was a member of both the Chinese Communist party and the Guomindang, a nationalist revolutionary group that had established a government at Nanjing under Chiang Kai-shek. (The Chinese Communists had been working with the Guomindang since 1924.)

In late 1926 Zhou had gone to Shanghai, the industrial center on the east coast of China. Since then, he had been organizing the leaders of the labor unions and the workers they represented to wrest control of the city from the local warlord.

On March 21, 1927, at the sound of the noon whistle, all transportation within Shanghai ground to a halt. An hour later attacks began on government, police, and communications headquarters.

Zhou Enlai (1898–1976) in Tianjin, just before his departure for Europe in 1920. Zhou's years abroad gave him a solid grounding in international politics that served him well when, in 1949, Mao Zedong (1893–1976) appointed him minister of foreign affairs for the People's Republic of China.

Zhou himself led 300 people in a successful attack on the post office. From there, he and his group of revolutionaries went on to capture police headquarters and the railway station. By 4:00 P.M. on the following day, the city was in the hands of Zhou's forces.

Zhou immediately proclaimed a "citizens' government" but knew that he needed additional support to retain control of the city. He expected Chiang Kaishek, who commanded a military force near the city, to provide that assistance. Chiang, however, had grown increasingly suspicious of the Communists within the Guomindang and now saw them as potential rivals. He seized this opportunity to destroy them. Chiang met with a group of rich merchants and criminal gang leaders of Shanghai. They agreed to support Chiang, just as they had previously cooperated with the warlord.

Early in the morning of April 12, the wail of a siren was heard throughout the city. It was the signal for Chiang's troops to enter Shanghai and commence operations against the Communists, who were based in the working-class districts. The first Communists they encountered—those on guard duty—were taken completely by surprise. Then, when the main body of the workers' militia responded to the emergency, Chiang's alliance with the Shanghai underworld began to pay immediate dividends. The gangsters, disguised as workers, murdered the union leaders, and, as a result, the workers' militia rapidly became an army without officers. The ill-equipped workers—"a ragamuffin army," in the words of one foreign newspaper correspondent—soon fell back. Their rifles and pistols were no match for the Guomindang's machine guns.

Zhou led the defense of the union headquarters, where the badly outnumbered workers soon realized that defeat was inevitable. Zhou managed to flee a few minutes before the building was overrun, but he was captured later in the day by Chiang's forces.

At this point the kindest fate Zhou might have expected was a speedy execution. Chiang had ordered savage reprisals, and an estimated 5,000

Our leadership was inexperienced, and we did not know either how to exploit our success or the tactics of retreat. The Shanghai workers and the peasants of the neighboring countryside were ready, but we did not have the machinery of cooperation ready. So Chiang was able to crush us.

—ZHOU ENLAI
speaking during the 1950s,
recalling the 1927
Shanghai insurrection

Communists were executed in the immediate aftermath of the Guomindang victory. "Heads rolled in ditches like ripe plums," reported one eyewitness. Others among Zhou's forces, however, were being tortured to reveal the names and hiding places of those who had organized or joined the revolt. But, as happened so often in Zhou's career, he managed to extricate himself from a seemingly impossible situation. The precise details of Zhou's escape from the clutches of the Guomindang remain unknown. According to one account of his escape, the chief prison officer had a brother whose life Zhou had once saved.

Although he was no longer a prisoner of the Guomindang, Zhou was not out of danger. Chiang had put a price of $80,000 on his head, and the police were circulating photographs of Zhou at the railway stations. Accordingly, Zhou shaved off his bushy eyebrows and grew a beard. He then boldly tested the effectiveness of his disguise by applying for the one document that would best guarantee his

Shanghai's Fuzhou Road was one of the city's busiest commercial thoroughfares and the scene of fierce fighting in 1927.

"Heads rolled in ditches like ripe plums," said one eyewitness as Chiang's Nationalist forces massacred thousands of Communists and sympathetic workers in the aftermath of the Shanghai insurrection.

safety—a Guomindang passport. Shortly after receiving his passport, Zhou left Shanghai aboard a train bound to the west for Wuhan, where he would join the other Communist leaders.

The cost of the Shanghai insurrection had been high. Chiang's execution of the city's top Communists was only the beginning of a wider campaign of systematic murder. During the weeks that followed, the Guomindang forces massacred thousands of workers suspected of being sympathetic toward the Communists, who were never to forget Chiang's treachery and the subsequent bloodbath.

Zhou, however, blamed himself for the disaster. Thirty years later he recalled, "I was responsible for leading the armed revolt, but I lacked experience and was weak in understanding political dynamics. I am an intellectual with a feudalistic family background. I had had little contact with the peasant-worker masses because I had taken no part in the economic process of production. My revolutionary career started abroad, with very limited knowledge about it, obtained from books only."

By that time, however, Zhou had helped lead a successful revolution and was premier, the second most powerful official, of the most populous country in the world.

Zhou Enlai was born in the town of Huaian on March 5, 1898. Huaian, in the rich, rice-growing Yangzi valley region of central eastern China, is located on the Grand Canal, which connects the Yangzi and Yellow rivers—China's largest waterways.

Zhou's family, however, were not farmers or laborers—something that would cloud his career as a communist revolutionary. Zhou described himself as coming from a "bankrupt mandarin family." Mandarins were Chinese who had passed the state examinations that made them eligible for government service. One of the privileges accorded them was that they never had to do physical labor. In later years Zhou commented on his father (to whom he was never close) and the system that produced a class of mandarins while millions sweated to eke out a living from the soil: "If it were not corruption, where could he have got the money for his long robes and his house?"

Zhou's father, Zhou Yinen, had passed the state examinations in the year of his son's birth. Thus, Zhou was given the name Enlai, meaning "coming of grace," in hopes that a government appointment would soon follow for his father. Though well-educated, Zhou's father had little social or professional ambition. In fact, he was content to serve in one petty clerkship after another and to spend what little money he earned on rice wine.

Zhou's mother, Wan Donger, a beautiful and cultivated woman, was also from a distinguished family. She was skilled in traditional Chinese art forms, such as painting and calligraphy, and was also extremely well read. Unfortunately for Zhou, Wan Donger's father died the day after Zhou's birth. Wan Donger was so overwhelmed by grief that depression rendered her incapable of caring for the boy.

About four months after his birth, the infant Zhou was brought to the home of his Uncle Yigan, an elder brother of his father. Yigan, who was seriously ill, was about to die childless—a prospect that to this day particularly disturbs Chinese men, since ancestry is traced through the male line in China. The importance attached by the Chinese to maintaining the family line had also given rise to a custom whereby a childless couple could adopt a male relative. In some cases, such adoptions were not made simply because a couple was childless; they often reflected another common Chinese tradition, whereby the offspring of ineffectual parents would be looked after by responsible relatives. While Wan Donger's shortcomings as a parent can at least be partially explained by her grief at the death of her father, her husband's inadequacies were of a different order. Zhou Yinen had always been irresponsible and lazy. Thus it was, in accordance with several Chinese traditions, that Zhou found himself in a new home. (Zhou was not actually very far from his real mother and father; the houses of the two families were close together in the family compound.)

Chiang's Nationalists, pictured here, fought savage battles with Zhou's Communists in Shanghai in 1927 as both groups sought to wrest control of the city from the local warlord who ruled it.

At the dock area of Tianjin in the late 1890s the preferred mode of transporting goods was by wooden wheelbarrow. At the time, the Boxers were engaged in their ill-fated attempt to rid China of foreign merchants and missionaries.

Zhou became devoted to his aunt and foster mother, Chen. An unconventional, strong-willed woman, she showered affection on the boy, telling him classical stories of ancient China and imaginative tales of myth and legend. Even after Chen remarried and had a son of her own, Zhou remained her favorite.

One of Chen's typically unconventional ideas was that Chinese children should be exposed to Western education. She paid a Christian missionary to teach Zhou and her natural son, Zhou Enzhu, at home. As a result, Enlai learned the rudiments of English and developed an interest in the world beyond China that later set him apart from many other Chinese leaders.

Zhou was also taught the venerable Chinese arts of painting and calligraphy. He became acquainted with the classic texts of Confucianism, an ethical and moral system based on the teachings of the ancient Chinese philosopher Confucius. Just to learn written Chinese, with its thousands of different characters, was a task that could take years to master. Although Zhou was unimpressed by most of the traditional subjects, he retained a lifelong love of Chinese poetry.

Zhou spent part of each year at Shaoxing, in Zhejiang province, about 300 miles south of Huaian. The ancestral home of the Zhou family was there, with its Hundred Year Hall, which held five generations of Zhous. It was at the Hundred Year Hall that the living family members paid respects to their ancestors. Devotion and respect for ancestors was one of the most important of the Confucian traditions. Their long list of ancestors was a source of pride to the Zhou family.

When Zhou was nine, he lost both Chen and Wan Donger. It was clear which of them he regarded as his real mother. "My aunt," he said, "became my real mother when I was a baby. I did not leave her for even one day until I was ten years old—when she and my natural mother both died." (In China, a baby is considered to be one year old on the day it is born. So Zhou counted himself as 10 years old when by Western methods of counting age, he was nine.) For the next two years, an elderly servant looked after him in the family compound.

When Zhou was 12, another of his uncles took him to live in the northeastern province of Manchuria. Here he was enrolled in the Dongguan Primary School, in the city of Shenyang.

Manchuria was far different from the fertile Yangzi valley. Its winters were fierce and its summers short. The people ate different food—not rice (the staple food of the southern Chinese), but millet (a less favored type of grain). Zhou also looked different from the northern children, and his schoolmates called him "the little Southerner."

At the Dongguan Primary School, which was run by Protestant missionaries, Zhou continued to learn traditional Chinese subjects as well as Western ones. It was in Shenyang that Zhou became aware

> *Without her care I would not have been able to cultivate any interest in academic pursuits.*
> —ZHOU ENLAI
> speaking about Chen, his foster mother

of the new forces that were then at work in Chinese society, and of the efforts that were being made to turn China into a modern nation. When the headmaster of the school asked why they were studying, Zhou answered, "So that China can rise up."

In the 19th century, China, which had long believed its civilization superior to all others, suffered some rude awakenings. Western nations used their superior military might to open the country to foreign trade and influence. In the wake of a series of military defeats, China lost the island seaport of Hong Kong to the British and relinquished legal jurisdiction in parts of some coastal cities to Great Britain and several other Western powers. (Those parts of the coastal cities where Chinese law did not apply were known as "concessions.") Then, in 1894, China was further humiliated by its defeat in a war with Japan. The reigning Manchu dynasty seemed unable to halt China's decline.

At the end of the 19th century a secret society, known as the Boxers, was formed to drive foreigners out of China. In 1900 the Boxers led a rebellion that threatened the foreign embassies in Beijing, the Chinese capital. A multinational military force landed in China and captured the city. The Chinese government was forced to pay a large amount of money to the governments of the occupying powers.

The Manchu leaders then attempted to modernize the country. The public examination system was abolished, efforts were made to reform the schools and the legal system, and the Manchu ruler promised to institute a form of constitutional government. However, the reforms carried out by the Manchus failed to satisfy their critics, and in 1911 China was convulsed by revolution. On February 12, 1912, the last Manchu emperor abdicated, and China was declared a republic.

Zhou and most of his schoolmates were delighted at the news. In a gesture of defiance, the jubilant youngster cut off his pigtail. (Ever since establishing control over China early in the 17th century, the Manchus had required all Chinese males to wear pigtails as a sign of submission to their rule.) At age 15, when he graduated, Zhou wrote a school

Going to Manchuria had two good points: first, it toughened my body. When I was in school, regardless of whether it was summer or winter, I wanted to go outside and strengthen my body, weak from studying. The other good point was sorghum. My living habits changed. My bones grew. My stomach toughened. It all made my body able to cope with years of struggle and intense work.
—ZHOU ENLAI
on moving to Manchuria at
the age of 12

friend: "Keep this in mind everywhere: when China soars over the world I would like us to meet again."

In 1913 Zhou passed the entrance examination for the Nankai Middle School in Tianjin. The school's reputation for nonconformism alarmed Zhou's family, but, in defiance of their wishes, he enrolled anyway. Fortunately, he had an aunt in Tianjin who agreed to let him live with her. Another uncle was found to pay the school's fees. Such were the advantages of having a large, extended family.

The principal of the Nankai Middle School was a Chinese Christian named Dr. Zhang Boling, who strongly believed in academic excellence. As a result, the curriculum was very demanding. Zhou was an excellent student and would later recall: "During my last two years at Nankai Middle School I received no help from my family. I lived on a scholarship which I won as best student in my class."

Because he was smaller than many of the other students, Zhou was at first taunted for his "daintiness." This problem was remedied when he befriended a very tall and athletic student named Wu

Chinese refugees in Shanghai during the 1930s. With China's economy still relatively backward and famine ravaging large areas of the country, many Chinese faced starvation. Because Zhou's father was a mandarin and thus eligible for government service, Zhou and his family were spared this fate.

Dager, with whom he shared a desk. Wu, a champion wrestler, became Zhou's protector.

It was during his time at the Nankai Middle School that several of the personal traits that were to characterize Zhou as an adult first began to emerge. His scholastic success was partly the result of extremely hard work. Zhou would study late into the night while the other students were asleep. He found that he could get by with as little as three hours sleep each night.

Zhou's organizing ability also became apparent during this period. He founded a group called the Respect Work and Enjoy Company Society, which was designed to give students an opportunity to make new friends and to exchange and discuss books and ideas.

Zhou also developed some acting ability at the Nankai Middle School. Dr. Boling, an ardent devotee of the theater, encouraged Zhou to get involved in the school's productions. As it was a boys' school, there was a need for someone to play the female parts. Zhou's high-pitched voice and his delicate, almost girlish features made him a natural choice for such roles.

He had too many women's airs about him. He liked to dress up and go on stage. That kind of person makes me feel sick.
—a classmate of Zhou's, discussing Zhou's portrayal of women's roles in school plays

Zhou's acting ability and his keen sense of drama would prove valuable assets in his future career as a diplomat. Decades later, one of Zhou's colleagues stated: "He is the greatest actor I have ever seen. He would laugh one moment and cry the next, and make all his audience laugh and cry with him. But it is all acting!"

Zhou's memories of his years at the Nankai Middle School would always be tinged with nostalgia. He never failed to call Dr. Boling whenever he was in Tianjin—even when he was hiding from the authorities. Dr. Boling was an important influence on Zhou, and the two men remained friends for life. Zhou later wrote: "I still thank the Nankai Middle School for that enlightening basic education that enabled me to pursue knowledge further."

After graduation, Wu Dager received a scholarship to a university in Japan. Wu persuaded other friends to contribute money so that Zhou could study there as well. After deciding to accept Wu's offer of assistance, Zhou wrote a poem suggesting that he still was uncertain about what to do with his life:

Song of the Grand River sung,
I head resolute for the East.
In vain I've searched all the schools
For clues to a better world.
By ten years' driving study
I'll make my breakthrough,
Or else die a hero
Who dared to tread the sea.

Zhou arrived in Japan in September 1917. Although Wu was in Kyoto, Zhou went to the Japanese capital, Tokyo. He enrolled in a course in Japanese so that he could enter the university, but never finished it. Finally, he accepted Wu's invitation to come to Kyoto to live with him and his wife.

In Kyoto, Zhou became acquainted with the work of Professor Kawakami Hijame, who was the publisher of a left-wing magazine called *Social Problems Research*. Kawakami's publication introduced Zhou to the political and economic theories of Karl

Japanese forces crossing the Yalu River during the First Sino-Japanese War (1894–95). China's defeat was one of the major humiliations the country endured during a half century of foreign aggression.

The Empress Dowager Tz'u-hsi (1835–1908), who entered the imperial court as a concubine, ruled China for 40 years during a period of great domestic challenges and increasing exploitation of the country by foreign powers.

Marx, the 19th-century German social philosopher whose writings form the basis of communism. Marx believed that capitalism (the economic system based on private enterprise) contained within itself the seeds of its own destruction and that it would eventually be replaced by communism, the social order in which the workers own the means of production—the land and the factories. Marx held that worldwide communism was historically inevitable because both class war between capitalists and workers *and* the workers' victory over capitalism were also historically inevitable.

Kawakami's magazine greatly increased Zhou's interest in politics—an interest that soon sparked arguments with Wu, who was strongly opposed to Marxism. Wu believed that China could only begin to solve its problems once it had achieved national unity, and that such unity could only be achieved

Yuan Shikai (1859–1916), the first president of the Republic of China. Yuan's strong military backing enabled him to assume control even though the revolutionaries favored Sun Yat-sen (1866–1925). He died in 1916 after his attempt to have himself named emperor failed.

The Empress Dowager's counselors, pictured here, were responsible for the government's dealings with foreigners. Particular points of concern for these men were the "scramble for concessions" by Western traders and the Western-influenced treaty system for settling disputes.

by a single, powerful leader. Zhou was convinced that positive change depended on educating the people.

In 1919 events in China persuaded Zhou that he should return home. During World War I, which lasted from 1914 to 1918, Japan had been allied with Britain, France, and the United States against Germany. The Japanese had not only seized the German concessions in China but had also made demands on the Chinese government that made the country little more than a Japanese colony. When China entered the war on the Allied side, it had fully expected that the territory taken by the Japanese would be restored once the war was over. In particular, China wanted the return of the Shandong peninsula, which had been part of the German concessions.

Following the defeat of Germany, negotiations between the countries that had participated in the conflict were held at Versailles, in France. In 1919 news reached China that, under the terms of the Treaty of Versailles, Shandong was to become a Japanese dependency. The Chinese were outraged. Students in Beijing burned the house of the Chinese minister who signed the treaty. When

some of the protesters were arrested, further demonstrations were staged in other Chinese cities. This wave of protest became known as the May Fourth Movement.

During this period of unrest, Zhou received a letter from one of his friends in Tianjin. His friend wrote: "If even our country is about to disappear, what is the use of your studying?" Zhou decided to return to China, and Wu's wife sold a ring to pay for his passage.

Upon returning to Tianjin, Zhou quickly became an eager participant in the furious protest activity that was sweeping the city. He enrolled at Nankai University in Tianjin and began to compose provocative editorials for its daily newspaper. He emphasized the need for the reform of Chinese society and for opening the country to new ideas. When the pro-Japanese Shandong warlord had several members of a patriotic society murdered, the angry Zhou wrote: "Compatriots! The forces of darkness are forever increasing. . . . What must we do to defend against them? There must be preparation, there must be sacrifice."

Hsuan-t'ung (1906–67), China's "boy emperor," abdicated the throne on February 12, 1912, ending Manchu reign and 22 centuries of dynastic rule. The last years of the empire were marked by failure of the government's administration system, political infighting at court, and widespread uprisings throughout the country.

**Republican soldiers of the
Chinese army in 1917. China
had allied itself with Great
Britain, France, and the
United States against Germany in World War I, hoping
to recover the Shandong
peninsula, which had been a
German concession. When
the Treaty of Versailles
awarded Shandong to the
Japanese, mass protests
erupted in China.**

Zhou expended much time and energy organizing
meetings in support of the May Fourth Movement.
He arranged for a delegation of students to join a
national protest at Beijing. They were promptly
thrown into jail, so another student group from
Tianjin went to Beijing to demonstrate for their release. Hundreds marched outside the office of the
president of China for three days. They were beaten
by the police and their leader was arrested. Zhou
then led a third group to Beijing, where they sur-
rounded the police station. Finally, the government
conceded and announced that the imprisoned students would be freed. Zhou received much acclaim
for having organized what was undoubtedly a major
political victory.

Zhou now turned his attention to combining the
separate protest groups into a single, more effective
organization. He started the Awakening Society,
which welcomed women as well as men into its
ranks.

Zhou's speech at the first meeting of the society
demonstrated that he was now familiar with *The
Communist Manifesto* and other works by Marx. He
declared: "All of us here today have been roused by

the new trend of thought of the twentieth century, and have become aware that the fundamental solution for Chinese society is to uproot and transform all those things which are incompatible with modern evolution: militarism, the capitalist class, powerful cliques, bureaucrats, sexual discrimination, the feudal grading of human relationships. . . ." Although he was not yet a communist, Zhou sympathized with many of Marx's ideas.

Developments similar to those taking place in Tianjin were now occurring in many other Chinese cities. In Changsha, the capital of Hunan province, a young man named Mao Zedong had founded an organization called the New People's Study Society.

One of the women who joined Zhou's Awakening

The Awakening Society, whose members are shown here, was formed by Zhou in 1919 in order to combine the various protest groups associated with the May Fourth Movement. Zhou is standing at the far right; third from the right in the first row is Deng Yingchao, a student activist whom Zhou would later marry.

An early picture of Mao Zedong. Mao and Zhou led the famous Long March of 1934–35 and 15 years later became the leaders of the People's Republic of China.

Demonstration in Beijing, April 1920, calling for a boycott of Japanese and British goods. The protests were part of the May Fourth Movement against the great powers' unfair treatment of China. Zhou returned to China from France so he could take part in the protests.

Society was Deng Yingchao, a student at the First Girls' Normal School in Tianjin. Although she was only 15, Deng was active in organizing protests in the May Fourth Movement. Her political relationship with Zhou would eventually blossom into romance.

Zhou's activities eventually brought him under police scrutiny. The student newspaper was shut down after the police raided its offices. In January 1920 Zhou was arrested in a demonstration. In prison, he organized a hunger strike, while students demonstrated outside, demanding his re-

lease. These actions forced the authorities to bring him to trial.

In August 1920 Zhou, thin from his prison ordeal, used the trial to present his political views, and even scolded the judge for his lack of patriotism. Zhou and his fellow defendants were sentenced to the time they had already served, and released.

It was now apparent to Zhou, and to his colleagues, that he was an exceptionally able political organizer. He had found his vocation. For the rest of his life he would devote his amazing energy and talents to the goal of transforming China.

Zhou following his release from jail in 1920. His role as a leader of student demonstrations led to his arrest; after a hunger strike and a highly publicized trial, Zhou was released—a major triumph that is thought to have cemented his commitment to political activism.

2

Professional Revolutionary

After leaving prison in 1920, Zhou sailed from Shanghai on a steamer bound for France, where he planned to enroll in a university. It was in Europe that Zhou made an ideological commitment to communism that was to give shape and meaning to his life. His increasing familiarity with the tenets of Marxism emerges very clearly from much that he wrote during this period. In a letter to the Awakening Society he declared: "We should believe in the theory of communism and in the two great principles of class revolution and the dictatorship of the proletariat."

Marx would have been surprised to learn that the major countries to adopt communism were Russia and China, where the practice of democracy was untried and where the majority of the population were not industrial workers, but peasants. Marx viewed advanced, industrial societies—capitalist democracies—as the natural forerunners of the communist order. Industrial workers in such democracies were generally better educated than their rural counterparts. They could, therefore, more easily be made to understand exactly how the capital-

Karl Marx (1818–83), German social philosopher whose ideas on communism were gradually embraced by Zhou. Marx was very critical of Chinese civilization and was said to feel that China, not being an advanced industrial society, was one of the least likely places for a communist revolution to occur.

Sun Yat-sen, leader of the 1911 revolution that overthrew the Manchu dynasty, in 1922. At the time Sun was working from a power base in Canton, trying to end the period of warlord rule that followed after the death of Yuan Shikai.

ists exercised control over them. With a true understanding of the causes of their oppression, the workers would be in a position to take the class war to its ultimate conclusion and to break that control. With the overthrow of the capitalists, what Marx called the "dictatorship of the proletariat" would be realized. In effect, the working class would become the *new* ruling class.

In Marx's opinion, bringing about such changes in agrarian societies presented almost insuperable problems. He believed that, as a class, peasants were innately conservative and generally unreceptive to new ideas. In his writings he had stressed that the industrial workers of Russia would have to be educated politically before they could hope to overthrow the monarchy. Once the monarchy had been toppled, the emancipated workers would face the herculean task of educating the peasants. Marx did not exaggerate the size of the problem. Many modern historians believe that the nature, beliefs, characteristics, and conditions of the Russian peasantry barely changed between the 16th and early 20th centuries. History had, in a manner of speaking, passed them by.

Marx realized that achieving communism in China would be even more difficult than in Russia. Life in rural China had changed very little in thousands of years. The kinds of rulers that China had known—warlords and emperors—had not created the sort of society in which progressive ideas could be expected to flourish. In fact, Marx was highly critical of Chinese civilization. It was, in his opinion, characterized by "overbearing prejudice, stupidity, learned ignorance, and pedantic barbarism."

Zhou, while fully aware of Marx's reservations concerning the prospects for revolution in China, realized that the success of the revolution that had taken place in Russia in 1917 meant that the communist order could be created, albeit with great difficulty, in a country where peasants comprised the majority of the population and where bourgeois democracy had never really been established. In Russia, professional communist revolutionaries led by Vladimir Lenin and his Bolshevik party had seized

Zhou Enlai is rather weak in his mastery of political theories, but he can summarize my ideas and represent them much better than I can. We depended on him to prepare all our public statements, either orally or in writing, because once he handled them they were sure to be accepted by all groups involved.

—a colleague of Zhou's
in Europe

power in the name of the workers following the abdication of the Russian *tsar*, or emperor. Thus, since 1917, Moscow had been the capital of the world communist movement.

While in Europe, Zhou received money from the Comintern (Communist International), an organization directed from Moscow to advance communism in other countries. He also received money from financial backers in China and earned money by working as a European correspondent for several Chinese newspapers.

Despite his radical ideas and activities, Zhou kept his middle-class habits of dress and lifestyle. He had his photograph taken and copied onto a postcard which he sent to his friend Wu, still in Kyoto. Zhou's message on the card was: "Paris is beautiful! Many friends, many sights. Would you like to come?" Soon, when his political activities brought him under police surveillance, Zhou would be more discreet about distributing his photograph.

Zhou's intention to enroll in a university in France did not last very long. The call of political organizing proved stronger. The French and

A gathering of the French branch of the Chinese Communist Youth League in Paris in 1924; Zhou is fourth from left in the front row. One of the young Communists recruited by Zhou was Deng Xiaoping (b. 1904), second from right in the back row, who in 1981 became China's premier.

Chinese authorities had agreed to establish a university for Chinese students at Lyons. It had also been decided that only newly arrived, middle-class Chinese would be admitted. This policy was meant to keep the university free of political activists. In response, Zhou organized a demonstration. With Zhou at their head, hundreds of students marched from Paris to Lyons to protest the university's admissions policy. The French police arrested the demonstrators, about 100 of whom were later deported.

In 1921 Zhou joined the Chinese Communist party and soon became one of its most valued members. His responsibilities as a party worker fell into three categories. The first was recruitment. One of his Paris recruits was Deng Xiaoping, who in the 1980s became premier of the People's Republic of China. In Berlin, Zhou recruited Zhu De to the party. Zhu would eventually become one of the most important leaders of the Chinese revolutionary movement.

Zhou's second major task was writing for *Youth*, the journal of the Chinese Communist Youth League. His articles set forth the official party line on various issues. Zhou proudly sent some of his articles to Wu, who responded thus: "Our ideas were never compatible. Let us each develop his thinking in his own way but remain friends forever. Your elder brother, Wu." This was the end of the correspondence between the two former friends.

The third of Zhou's tasks was liaison work with other Chinese groups in Europe. The most important of these was the Guomindang, whose members were followers of Sun Yat-sen, the leader and guiding spirit of the 1911 revolution. The goal of the Guomindang was the creation of a strong, independent Chinese republic. Zhou sympathized with some of the Guomindang's aims, but felt that their proposals for social reform were insufficiently radical. As usual, Zhou was skilled at finding areas of agreement among the various groups with which he worked.

The friendships Zhou established in Europe were to be important in his later career. Many of the

> *He was a slender man of more than average height and with a face so striking that it bordered on the beautiful. Yet it was a manly face, serious and intelligent. Zhou was a quiet and thoughtful man, even a little shy.*
>
> —ZHU DE
> Chinese Communist leader, recalling his first impression of Zhou when they met in Paris

people he had recruited would become prominent revolutionaries. But now the party, pleased with his work, decided he would be more valuable within China itself. Zhou left Paris in June 1924.

The official Chinese government, to which other nations sent ambassadors, was in Beijing. Its power was severely limited, and the presidency tended to change hands at the whim of whichever warlord controlled the Beijing area.

In the south, in the city of Canton, a regime led by Sun Yat-sen and the Guomindang claimed to be the legal government of China. However, Sun's contention that he was the legal ruler of China was ignored by other countries. In an effort to gain foreign support for his cause, Sun turned to the government of the Union of Soviet Socialist Republics, as Russia was now known. The Soviet government declared that it was willing to cede the concessions that Russia had won from China in the 19th century. A Soviet adviser contacted Sun and agreed to help his forces with military and political training. (The Soviets were also working with the Beijing government.)

In January 1924, six months before Zhou's departure from Paris, the first Guomindang congress had been convened in Canton. The delegates to the congress decided that the Guomindang government would contract an alliance with the Soviet government, collaborate with the Chinese Communist party in domestic affairs, and work to increase its influence among the workers and peasants in the area surrounding Canton.

Zhou arrived back in China in August 1924 and went directly to Canton, where he was appointed secretary of the local Communist party. Zhou was also a member of the Guomindang. Another person with dual membership was Mao Zedong, whom Zhou met at this time and who was now running a political center called the Peasant Movement Training Institute.

Zhou was warned that the Chinese Communist party was to take care not to have its own revolutionary fervor diluted by its association with the Guomindang, whose political stance was not as rad-

The Nationalists opposed Communism partly for generational reasons. Most of them were older than the Communists who had come of age during the May Fourth Movement, when the West looked particularly bad and the Russian Revolution exerted powerful attraction. For the older generation, Russia remained just another country not to be trusted, and May Fourth was schoolboy rowdyism.
—ED HAMMOND
American historian

ical as that of the Communists.

In 1924 the Guomindang appointed Zhou to be deputy director of the political department at the Huangpu Military Academy, which had recently been established as the training ground for a new Chinese revolutionary army. The commandant at Huangpu was Sun's military lieutenant, Chiang Kai-shek, who had completed his training in the Soviet Union. Zhou himself had no military experience, but he learned quickly. He also worked to promote Marxist ideas among the students of the academy.

In 1925 the fledgling Guomindang army underwent its baptism of fire. The Eastern Expedition was launched to increase the Canton government's power over the entire province of Guangdong. In his capacity as political officer, Zhou had the task of trying to convince the local peasantry to support the campaign. Although the size of the Guomindang army was initially only 3,000 men, the support it received from the peasants enabled it to defeat the forces of the local warlord.

For Zhou, the year 1925 also brought great changes in his private life. Deng Yingchao, the young woman who had helped him organize the Awakening Society in Tianjin, came to Canton to attend a Guomindang conference. Deng was now a member of both the Communist party and the Guomindang. Shortly after her arrival in Canton, she and Zhou renewed their acquaintance. A few days later, they were married.

Marriages in China were traditionally arranged by the couple's parents. Zhou and Deng, however, had chosen each other. In place of the traditional ceremony, they repeated vows known as the "Eight Mutuals" before a small gathering of their closest friends. They declared that they would love each other, respect each other, help each other, encourage each other, consult each other, have consideration for each other, have confidence in each other, and have understanding for each other. Theirs was often cited as a model communist marriage.

The year 1925 also saw the death of Sun Yat-sen. Many members of his party had disapproved of his

Every day I went out, never knowing whether I would not be arrested. The police searched my house in the international settlement. Many good friends were killed and our work became impossible.
—DENG YINGCHAO
on underground life in
Shanghai, after Chiang
turned against the
Communists

decision to accept Communists into the Guomindang, but while he lived the alliance was respected. Shortly after Sun's death, Chiang, who strongly distrusted the Communists, became head of the Guomindang. The cohesion of the United Front—as the alliance between the Guomindang and the Communists was known—was about to be sorely tested.

On March 20, 1926, suspecting that the Communists were engaging in treasonable activities, Chiang ordered a crackdown at Huangpu. He relieved the Soviet advisers and the Communist political officers of their duties and imposed martial law. Zhou was placed under house arrest. Later that same day, Chiang, convinced that he had made a sufficient demonstration of his power, began to mollify the Soviet advisers and ordered the release of some of the Communists. However, it was now obvious that Chiang and his colleagues intended to run the Chinese revolution themselves.

In the wake of this incident, some Communists

A demonstration against foreigners, in Shanghai in 1925. During one such protest an international police unit killed twelve students, unleashing a wave of sentiment against foreigners that greatly increased support for the Communist and Nationalist movements.

wanted to go on the offensive against Chiang. Zhou, however, used his skills to try to keep the United Front intact. Zhou's efforts were influenced by orders from Joseph Stalin, the leader of the Soviet Union, who wanted the United Front to continue.

There were many people in the Guomindang who wanted to maintain the United Front, and even Chiang recognized that the Northern Expedition— a long-awaited campaign to extend Guomindang control over China—would not succeed without assistance from the Chinese Communists and the Soviet military advisers. Soon, Chiang reappointed Zhou to some of his posts and created a section for Communist cadets at the Huangpu academy.

The Northern Expedition got under way in July 1926, meeting with considerable success. By the end of the year the Guomindang army was at the Yangzi delta, about 700 miles north of Canton. This was the time when Zhou went to Shanghai, China's most modern and highly industrialized city, to prepare for its takeover by the Guomindang. His wife was there too, helping to organize. Although Zhou's efforts led to initial success, the Communists were promptly betrayed by Chiang, whose massacre of his former allies made a mockery of Stalin's assertions that "they [the Guomindang] have to be utilized to the end, squeezed out like a lemon, and then flung away."

At the end of July, Zhou went to Nanchang, where one of his early recruits, Zhu De, had retained his post as head of public security and deputy military commander of the left-wing Guomindang forces because it was not known that he was a Communist. With Zhu's help, Zhou secretly made plans for an uprising.

A short time later, the Communist leadership in Nanchang received new orders from Moscow. They were not to proceed unless they were sure of victory. Zhou and his colleagues discussed this latest development at considerable length, and Zhou threatened to resign unless the revolt took place as planned. Early in the morning of August 1, 1927, Zhou's forces went into action. The Communists won the first engagements of the day, but the sit-

First, unite Guangdong [the Nationalists' southern provincial base]; second, unite China; third, smash imperialism.

—ZHOU ENLAI
speaking in 1925, stressing the importance of unity between Nationalists and Communists

uation began to deteriorate when they learned that a hostile force led by General Zhang Fakui, who had originally agreed to help them, was fast approaching Nanchang. The Communist forces immediately withdrew from the city. Zhou retreated south, later finding refuge in Hong Kong. (Zhu De would eventually take part of his army to the base that Mao Zedong was to establish in northwestern China.)

At about the same time, Mao led a revolt—known as the Autumn Harvest uprising—in his native Hunan, in south central China. Its objective was to capture Changsha, but it did not succeed. At the end of the year, a Communist uprising in Canton also failed, and 4,000 Communist supporters were killed. The year 1927 had seen the failure of the strategy of local uprisings, and the decimation of the Chinese Communist party.

The situation of the Chinese Communists remained precarious for the next four years. Chiang continued his Northern Expedition, taking Beijing in June 1928. He established a new capital at Nanjing, where the Guomindang central executive committee announced the formation of a new government—the National Government of China. The Guomindang also proclaimed that it would be the only political party of the government. Chiang had moved the country toward unity, but he ruled in some areas with the tacit support of warlords. There were also pockets of Communist resistance.

During this period, Stalin, seemingly oblivious to the difficulties his Chinese allies were facing, ordered the Chinese Communists to build up the party and, at the same time, to organize revolts against Chiang's regime. Zhou was one of the party leaders who continued to obey the instructions of the Comintern. The uprisings demanded by Stalin were largely unsuccessful, and the Chinese party leaders had to take the blame for the failure of insurrections that many historians feel should never have been attempted at all. In 1931 Zhou publicly apologized for what he considered his own political deficiencies, declaring: "I call upon the whole Party to condemn my mistakes."

Despite his failures, Zhou kept a top position in

Zhou as a political commissar in the years following his return from France in 1924. After allying himself with Sun (who died in 1925) and then with Chiang, Zhou went underground in the late 1920s to escape capture during Chiang's purge of the Communists.

Refugees in 1926. Many Chinese peasants were displaced from their homes as a result of the Nationalist-Communist civil war in which the Guomindang attempted to "pacify" the Communists, who opposed Chiang's ascendancy.

the party—the only one of the Chinese leaders to do so. However, he seemed to lack the drive or ambition to take full control of party affairs. Although he exerted much influence behind the scenes, he was never to hold the position of party secretary, or chief. During this time Zhou was described by a friend as "a tireless worker who did not talk much." He dealt very calmly with complex affairs, both day and night. He took on both work and blame, disregarding criticism. He was responsible for handling most of the work concerned with dispersing comrades. This period also marked the beginning of his being treated with respect by comrades in general and the growth in importance of his status. In some circles Zhou was called "man of iron."

Zhou spent much of this period at the party headquarters in Shanghai. The city offered the party (which was once more operating underground) a certain safety because of the foreign concessions, where the Communists could hide beyond the reach of the Chinese police.

Zhou's aunt and uncle were still living in Shanghai, and Zhou and Deng adopted the lifestyle of a middle-class couple. Zhou told his relatives that he was waiting for an appointment to a government post. He observed the traditional role of a dutiful Chinese family member. On the anniversary of the death of his grandfather, Zhou—as the eldest grandchild—directed the family memorial service. As was customary, pieces of yellow paper bearing messages for the dead ancestor were ritually burned. Zhou's aunt was so impressed by her nephew's careful observance of the ceremony that she said: "Zhou really knows all the rules. He does everything just right."

In 1931 Zhou, once again, narrowly escaped being captured by Chiang's forces. Gu Shunzhang, whom Zhou had appointed head of the party's secret service, was caught by the Nationalists. Under torture, Gu revealed the names of the Communist party leaders in Shanghai. Zhou, disguised as a monk, managed to escape the roundup that followed and boarded a steamer that took him down the coast. Before he left Shanghai, he showed the ruthless side of his nature by ordering the slaughter of Gu's family in retaliation for his confession, which Zhou regarded as an act of betrayal.

The party leadership now decided to relocate in a safer place. In some remote regions, the Commu-

> *Revolution is not a dinner party, nor an essay, nor a painting, nor a piece of embroidery; it cannot be advanced softly, gradually, carefully, considerately, respectfully, politely, plainly and modestly.*
> —MAO ZEDONG

Northern troops—a ragtag force of warlord cronies and others—take a last stand against Nationalist-Communist forces on the verge of entering Shanghai in 1927. Zhou oversaw the taking of the city only to have Chiang turn on him, forcing him to flee to Nanjing and, later, to Hong Kong.

Painting by artist Wang Shikuo depicting the formation of the Red Army. Mao (left) and Zhu De (1886—1976) forged the historic union between workers and peasants to form revolutionary troops in Jiangxi province in 1928.

nists had established special bases that they called *soviets*. The largest of these was headed by Mao Zedong.

Mao, who was growing increasingly skeptical of the conflicting and sometimes disastrous orders issued to the Chinese Communists by the Comintern, had by this time emerged as the party's most brilliant organizer of peasants. At his base in Jiangxi, he had built an army of nearly 100,000 men. For all his success, however, Mao had never been rewarded with a top post in the party. The distance of his base from Shanghai had allowed him to operate independently. Now, with the move of the party leadership to the Jiangxi Soviet in the fall of 1931, he had to submit to their decisions.

Most of the Chinese Communist leaders had been trained in Moscow. The members of the most important group within the leadership were known as "the 28 Bolsheviks." In November, the First All-China Soviet Congress was convened in Ruijin, a city in the Jiangxi Soviet. There, many of Mao's policies were denounced, among them his ideas of guerrilla warfare against the Guomindang. The 28 Bolsheviks favored more orthodox military campaigns. Zhou agreed with them.

Zhou was appointed political commissar of the Red Army, as the Communists' armed forces were now known. He proposed that the Red Army be expanded through forced recruitment and then used to invade Nationalist territory. Mao, however, believed that such methods would alienate the peasants and that the peasants should be left alone to work their fields, producing food for the population in those areas already under Communist control.

Mao's strategy, which he had used with much success, was to lure Nationalist armies into his territory, where they were then harassed by small raiding parties. These hit-and-run tactics conserved manpower, bled the enemy's forces, and eventually forced them to withdraw. Using these methods, Mao's army had fought off three of Chiang's "extermination campaigns."

Mao also came into conflict with Zhou and the other party leaders on the question of land reform. Zhou followed the official party line, which, following precedents set in the Soviet Union, called for the elimination of the landlords and prosperous peasants. The thousands of people who fell into these two categories were to be herded into camps and their land distributed to the poor peasants. Mao

Chinese Nationalists march on Beijing, 1928. Shortly after Chiang's forces seized the city—and well after the collapse of the United Front with the Communists—Chiang proclaimed the Nationalist government of China, in which the Guomindang was to be the sole political party.

Nationalist troops lined up for inspection. Chiang continued his campaign against the Communists in the 1930s and, with the help of German military advisers, his troops forced the Communists into the famous retreat known as the Long March.

was convinced that this kind of upheaval could not be accomplished overnight or through a simple decree. His immediate concern was to keep the people in his territory well fed. Larger farms, he believed, were more efficient than small plots of land.

In 1934 Chiang launched a new campaign against the Communists. He secured the services of German military advisers and assembled a large body of troops. His strategy was to surround the Communist bases, thus blocking their lines of communication and preventing them from receiving food and medical supplies. When Mao responded to the situation by insisting on using his previous tactics, the Communist leadership removed him from his position as chairman of the central executive committee of the party and put him under house arrest. Calling for "victory or death," Zhou then supervised a full-scale Communist assault on the Nationalist army. But Chiang's forces were simply too strong. It became clear that the only way for the Communists to survive was to abandon their bases and attempt to escape.

In the fall of 1934, Zhou visited Mao to review the situation, and the two men quickly agreed that the

Communist forces had no choice but to withdraw—to put as much distance as possible between themselves and Chiang's armies. On October 16, 1934, there began the legendary retreat that has gone down in history as the Long March. More than 100,000 men, women, and children walked 6,000 miles, crossing mountains, rivers, forests, and swamps.

Zhou took with him nothing but the barest essentials: two blankets; a quilt; a change of clothes that doubled as a pillow; a brass ink vial; and a rectangular document case that held pencils, maps, a magnifying glass, and a compass. Each night Zhou would map out the route for the next day. He led the column that included the government and military headquarters staff, and the women and

Japanese troops in Shenyang, China, during a 1931 invasion launched to protect their "treaty rights." Japan went on to capture all of Manchuria, sparking increased public sentiment for the Nationalist government to stand up to the Japanese aggression.

children. His wife, Deng, was suffering from tuberculosis, and Zhou himself would become ill on the journey.

Many of the marchers died along the way: some drifted into the countryside, others became lost. When the Nationalists drew near, the Communists marched at night, tying white towels on their backs so that those behind could follow.

Early in 1935, the marchers arrived in Zunyi, a town in the northern part of Guizhou province. There, they stopped to hold a party conference that was to have enormous significance for the future of China. The party leadership discussed the mistakes that had been made in previous years. It was reported later that Zhou said: "[Mao] has been right all the time and we should listen to him." His support was decisive. Mao emerged from the conference as the head of the Chinese Communist party—a position he would hold for the rest of his life.

In supporting Mao at the party conference in Zunyi, Zhou demonstrated his ability to adapt in order to survive. We do not know what Zhou thought of Mao's subsequent decisions or his fitness to lead, but he never publicly challenged him again. In the wake of the conference, the two men began to establish what was to prove an extremely productive working relationship.

Zhou may have recognized in Mao a complement to his own personality. Whereas Zhou was urbane, came from a cultured mandarin family, and had considerable experience of the world beyond China's borders, Mao was from a peasant background and had never been outside the country. Between them, Mao and Zhou could draw upon a wealth and diversity of experience that would greatly assist them in their endeavors to turn their backward homeland into a world power.

During the Long March, Zhou insisted that the party leaders share the hardships of their followers, just as Mao always maintained that even the highest official should be prepared to work alongside the peasants in the fields. It was widely known at the time that Chiang's troops were stealing from peasants living in the territories occupied by the

Wall poster seen in Nanjing in 1937 depicts a Chinese soldier leaping over the Great Wall in a victory charge against the Japanese. Though the legend read "Recover lost territories, relieve the Manchurian countrymen," Chinese forces were quickly routed by the Japanese and fled the city.

Nationalists. As a result, thousands of peasants grew disillusioned with the Nationalist government and many began to support the Communists. Zhou wanted to gain the trust and support of the peasant masses, and therefore ordered that they be treated fairly and honestly. When one of Zhou's bodyguards found some cornmeal and eggs, he brought the food to Zhou, who asked if he had paid for it. The bodyguard said that he had not because he had been unable to find the owner. Zhou insisted that the man return and pay for what he had taken, and then took the food and distributed it.

When the marchers came to Luding, on the Dadu River, they discovered that the planks of the bridge across the river had been badly damaged by Nationalist shelling. Some Communist troops had already picked their way across, but only with great difficulty and very slowly. Zhou realized that it would be impossible to sustain the pace of the march unless the bridge was repaired. Zhou and his men had

Soviet officer Mikhail Borodin (center; 1884–1951) was Sun Yat-sen's personal adviser and the Comintern's main representative in Canton in the mid-1920s. Zhou would later apologize publicly for following Moscow's advice, which many historians feel led to many Communist defeats at the hands of Chiang (third from left).

Zhou (third from right) with other Red Army commanders in 1933. For a time the Red Army was able to hold its own against Chiang's forces, but amid differences over military strategy and under relentless pressure from the Guomindang, the Communists were put on the run.

to inch their way across, repairing and replacing the planks as they went. Zhou told his bodyguard how to cross the bridge: "You have to be careful, keep your eyes on the opposite bank, and do not look down at the ravine far below."

Shortly after this incident, Zhou became seriously ill with a liver infection and had to be carried along on a stretcher. Although his body was swollen and there was no medication available, Zhou kept to the punishing schedule that he had maintained since the beginning of the march, often staying up all night to plan the next day's route.

When the marchers came to the snowy Jiajin Mountains, they found themselves struggling through storms in which hailstones as big as walnuts fell. For many southern Chinese, who were unused to such cold, this part of the march proved fatal. But the most difficult part of the trek was through the grasslands near Tibet. Zhou recalled it as "the darkest time." Food was so scarce that the marchers were forced to eat their belts, boiling them until they were soft and then throwing greens and herbs into the pot. Thus they concocted what Zhou described as "the soup of three delicacies."

Crossing the grasslands was the last great hurdle. In October 1935 the survivors of the Long March arrived in Shaanxi province, where a major Red Army base had been in existence for several years. Shaanxi was one of the most poverty-stricken areas in all China. Zhou described it thus: "Peasants in Shaanxi are extremely poor, their land very unproductive. . . . In Jiangxi and Fujian people brought bundles with them when they joined the Red Army on the Long March; here they do not even bring chopsticks; they are utterly destitute."

It was to the abolition of such poverty and destitution that the Chinese Communists had dedicated their lives. Although much had been accomplished, there were many more years of trial and hardship ahead. The Long March would prove to have been but one stage of a difficult and demanding journey.

Zhou just after the Long March, 1935. That "strategic retreat"—a grueling, 6,000-mile trek by 100,000 men, women, and children to Shaanxi province, out of reach of Chiang's army—saw Mao's emergence, with Zhou's support, as the main Communist leader.

3

War

For the sake of our revolution
we must be very patient. For
the sake of our revolution
we can play the role of a
concubine, even of
a prostitute.
—ZHOU ENLAI
speaking in 1927

The survivors of the Long March were quartered in the thousands of caves in the Shaanxi hills, first in Baoan, then in Yan'an. Visiting American journalist Edgar Snow, whom Zhou first met during this period, described them thus: "They were not caves in the Western sense. Cool in summer, warm in winter, they were easily built and easily cleaned. . . . Some of them were many-roomed edifices gaily furnished and decorated with stone floors and high-ceilinged chambers, lighted through rice-paper windows opened in the walls of earth. . . ."

Life was hard in the Shaanxi caves, but the fellowship and sense of purpose that had been engendered on the Long March created a feeling of camaraderie among the survivors, most of whom, in later years, looked back on the experience with nostalgia. They began to reorganize the army and to recruit peasants from throughout the province.

Zhou's wife, Deng, counseled local women in practical matters such as childcare, family problems, and the need to eliminate footbinding. (Footbinding was an ancient Chinese custom in which the feet of female infants were wrapped tightly in cloth and bound continually through adolescence in order to

Zhou in Yan'an in 1937. The Japanese invasion of China that year prompted the Communists and the Nationalists to form a new (and uneasy) alliance, with Zhou serving as Chiang's military adviser. Zhou saw the move as a way to make great political gains among the Chinese populace.

The Chinese Red Army in Shaanxi, the site of a major Communist base, in 1935. Following the Long March to this impoverished northern province, the Communists began to regroup, enlist new supporters, and plot their next moves.

Feet disfigured by footbinding, an ancient Chinese custom. The feet of many Chinese girls were wrapped tightly with cloth so as to inhibit growth and thus achieve the goal of small, delicate, "beautiful" feet. Zhou's wife campaigned actively for an end to the practice.

inhibit growth. Small feet were considered delicate and highly desirable by traditional Chinese standards of beauty.)

Deng's health had improved dramatically following the end of the Long March. "Strange to say," she later wrote, "after a year's extremely strenuous life in the Long March, I was cured without any special medical treatment." During their time in Yan'an, Zhou and his wife adopted a daughter, Sun Weishi, one of the thousands of children whose parents had been killed by the Guomindang or the warlords and whom the party had taken into its care.

As always, Zhou balanced an enormous workload with an active social life. He was an excellent bridge player and an expert dancer. His urbanity and sophistication often surprised foreigners meeting him for the first time. Edgar Snow, who was quite astonished when Zhou greeted him in English, described him thus: ". . . of slender stature, of medium height, with a slight wiry frame, boyish in his appearance despite his long black beard, and with large, warm, deep-set eyes. There was certainly a kind of magnetism about him that seemed to derive from a curious combination of shyness, personal charm and a complete assurance of command."

Although Shaanxi served as a sanctuary for the Communists, their position was still vulnerable. In an effort to strengthen the Communist enclave against both the Nationalists and the Japanese, Zhou was sent to negotiate an agreement with the warlord who controlled the region, Zhang Xueliang, commander of China's Northeastern Army. Zhang, who was popularly known as the Young Marshal, was from Manchuria, which had been conquered by the Japanese in 1931.

Zhou and the Young Marshal were both of the opinion that the Chinese had to unite in order to counter the Japanese threat. The joint proclamation that the two men devised at their meeting constituted a stirring appeal to Chinese patriotism and contained such memorable phrases as "Chinese do not fight Chinese" and "Inhuman is he who slays his own brother to feed the wolf."

News of the partnership between Zhou and the

This iron smelter in a hand grenade plant manufactured weapons for the Red Army in the 1930s.

Young Marshal greatly disturbed Chiang, who believed that national unity was only to be achieved by suppressing the Communists. Only when this had been done, he believed, would China be strong enough to fight the Japanese. "The Japanese aggression," he had said, "comes from without and can be compared to a disease of the skin, while the bandit [Communist] rebellion, working from within, is really a disease of the heart."

In December 1936 Chiang flew to Xi'an, where the Young Marshal had established his headquarters. Chiang planned to tell Zhang that unless the Northeastern Army commenced operations against the Red Army bases in Yan'an immediately, he would order Zhang's forces out of Xi'an and give the job of crushing the Yan'an Communists to other Nationalist formations. Negotiations between the two men had barely begun when, on December 12, 1936, some of the Northeastern Army's more independent-minded officers took Chiang prisoner. Their intention was to force him to agree to fight the Japanese more aggressively.

Chiang's captors had not revealed their intentions to the Young Marshal, who was stunned by this unexpected development. Uncertain about how to handle the situation, he turned to Zhou for advice.

Both Zhou and Mao were naturally delighted to hear that Chiang had been captured. But they were also aware of the fact that the Soviet government would be greatly displeased were Chiang to come to any harm. The Soviets had consistently held that Chinese unity was of the utmost importance and that Chiang was indispensable to its preservation. As he had on many previous occasions, Stalin intervened personally, sending the Chinese Communist leaders a telegram in which he ordered them to secure Chiang's unconditional release. The Soviet dictator was firmly convinced that the capture of Chiang was a Japanese plot. Stalin and his colleagues also believed that the Japanese would be quick to take advantage of the chaos that would result from Chiang's death, overrunning more Chinese territory and drawing closer to the eastern

> *What set Zhou apart from the other Communists was that he was, by education, a larger man; and by temperament, an elastic man.*
> —THEODORE WHITE
> American writer

borders of the Soviet Union.

Zhou understood that it would not be easy to convince the Young Marshal to agree with the Soviet assessment of the situation. Before departing for Xi'an, he warned his comrades that he was in no position to dictate policy to Zhang. "We alone cannot decide what to do," he said. "The attitude of the Young Marshal . . . has to be taken into account."

There were many among both Zhou's colleagues and the senior commanders of the Northeastern Army who wanted Chiang executed. However, Zhou managed to convince them that the situation should be used to persuade Chiang to cooperate with the Red Army and to force him to allow the Communists to participate in the struggle against the Japanese.

No definitive account is available of the meeting between Zhou and Chiang at Xi'an. Zhou remarked later that he said to Chiang, "I am your student. So long as we are fighting Japanese, anything you say

Chiang with Zhang Xueliang (far left, bottom), the commander of China's Northeastern Army, who was popularly known as the Young Marshal. When Chiang was kidnapped by some of Zhang's officers in late 1936, Zhou secured his release in exchange for a promise to end the suppression of the Communists.

This depiction of the Japanese aggression against China in 1937 comes from a French humor magazine.

will be acceptable to us." Chiang supposedly replied, "All the time we have been fighting I often thought of you. I remembered even during the civil war that you have worked well for me. I hope we can work together again."

After the meeting, Zhou cabled Mao: "Chiang Kai-shek is ill. When I saw him, he indicated that the suppression of Communists will stop, there will be an alliance with the Red Army to resist Japan. . . . Judging from what has happened, there was a real change in Chiang Kai-shek's attitude. . . . When he was about to leave, Chiang said . . . 'From now on I will never engage in the suppression of Communists.' "

Zhou persuaded the Young Marshal of Chiang's

sincerity, and Chiang was released on Christmas Day, 1936. The Communists and the Nationalists then set about negotiating for the resurrection of the United Front. During the negotiations, Zhou frequently traveled between Xi'an and Yan'an to consult with Mao. The talks dragged on for several months, accomplishing very little. Then, in July 1937, the Japanese launched a full-scale attack on China. This move made the United Front a necessity and an agreement was quickly reached. In return for Communist recognition of Chiang as leader of China, the Red Army was allowed to operate as a legitimate element of the nation's armed forces. It would not, however, be fully integrated with those forces. It would be known as the Chinese Eighth Route Army, taking its orders from the government in Nanjing. Also under the terms of this agreement, the Communist-controlled territories became the Northwest Border Region and were accepted as a political unit of China. In addition, the Communists agreed to suspend some of their reforms, including the confiscation of landlords' holdings.

Zhou, Mao, and Zhu De as they appeared in 1939, when their Communist forces were battling the Japanese.

Zhou began to travel back and forth from Yan'an to the various Nationalist bases. During this time, he acquired a reputation as a moderate. He was a first-rate spokesman and ambassador for the Communists, charming almost everyone who met him, from generals and diplomats to journalists.

The war went badly for the Chinese. Beijing quickly fell to the Japanese, who then swept through northern China, taking Shanghai and moving toward Nanjing, the Nationalist capital. In December 1937 the Nationalist government fled the city. When the Japanese troops arrived, they engaged in an orgy of looting and plunder. The "rape of Nanjing" shocked the world and was largely instrumental in persuading the government of the United States that the Japanese were fast becoming a serious threat to American interests in the Far East.

Zhou spent most of 1938 at the new Nationalist capital, Wuhan. In addition to his liaison work, he

Devastation and an infant's agonized face tell the story in late 1937, when the Japanese seized Shanghai and Chinese forces retreated to the south. The Japanese had already captured Beijing and much of northern China and would soon take Nanjing, the capital.

helped edit a Communist newspaper. In an editorial, he wrote: "[Chiang] is the rightful and the only person to lead the entire nation to victory, because of his revolutionary experience and dedication." Zhou's public support for Chiang was so enthusiastic that many people began to believe he might defect to the Nationalists.

Deng, Zhou's wife, had been in Beijing when the Japanese attacked. Edgar Snow managed to smuggle her out of the city, disguised as a nursemaid, and she joined her husband in Wuhan, where they set up house in a luxurious villa, the most comfortable accommodation they would ever know.

In the fall of 1938 the Japanese marched on Wuhan. The Nationalists abandoned the city and established a new capital at Chongqing, in Sichuan province. There, Zhou and his wife took up residence in a bomb-damaged house at the end of a dark, damp alley. Despite the fact that the United Front was now officially in operation, Zhou was kept under surveillance by the Nationalist secret service.

During his time in Wuhan, Zhou received many visitors, both foreign and Chinese. He also fostered ties with possible non-communist allies. To American visitors (who appeared to be his favorites), Zhou stressed that a postwar Chinese Communist government would be eager to establish friendly relations with the United States.

Something of the humor and diplomacy for which Zhou was by now becoming renowned is revealed by an incident that took place when he was entertaining American writer Theodore White. Zhou's staff had arranged an elaborate dinner for White at a local restaurant. They had ordered a suckling pig, which took hours to prepare. White, however, became embarrassed the moment he was confronted with the meal. He explained that, as a Jew, he was not allowed to eat pork. From the astonished glances of his hosts, White realized that the Chinese had been entirely unaware of this. He also realized that it was impossible for them to offer a substitute. According to White, Zhou picked up his chopsticks and gestured to the dish on the table, saying, "Teddy, this is China. Look again. See . . . it looks

Zhou plotting strategy in 1943. As World War II raged, Zhou—despite the collapse of the alliance with the Guomindang in 1941—continued to denounce the fratricide and worked for unity against the Japanese. One biographer says he was the "conscience of China's political system."

Portrait of a Chinese guerrilla, 1944. The United States, also battling the Japanese, considered the Communists a more potent fighting force than the Nationalists, who were poorly disciplined and had begun to resort to brutality, particularly against civilians.

to you like a pig, but in China this is not a pig—this is a duck." White laughed, picked up his own chopsticks, and ate what he later described as ". . . my first mouthful of certified pig."

In the spring of 1939 Chiang approved Zhou's request that the Communist forces in Jiangxi province be legitimized by the Nationalists and reconstituted as the New Fourth Army. Thus, the Communists gained a major military base in southern central China. Zhou then conducted a tour of inspection, visiting Communist formations in Anhui, Zhejiang, and Jiangxi provinces. Shortly thereafter, the New Fourth Army commenced operations against the Japanese in the Yangzi region. Although the Communists' guerrilla tactics proved reasonably successful, they did not suffice to dislodge the Japanese completely.

Early in 1941, Chiang once again turned on the Chinese Communists. His forces attacked the New Fourth Army. This latest betrayal seemed particularly despicable to Zhou, who had been largely responsible for the creation of the New Fourth Army and had done everything he could to maintain cordial relations with Chiang.

Even though he realized that the United Front was now damaged beyond repair, Zhou continued to work for unity against the Japanese. In a speech that he gave in Chongqing in the spring of 1941, he declared: "This is our country. Whatever has happened to cause that fratricidal tragedy must be forgotten. From now on we must look ahead. . . . The grave of my mother to whom I owe everything that I am and hope to be is in Japanese-occupied Zhejiang. How I wish I could just go back there once to clear the leaves on her grave—the least a prodigal son who has given his life to revolution and his country could do for his mother."

After 1943, Zhou spent most of his time in Yan'an. In 1944, on the orders of American President Franklin D. Roosevelt, an American military mission was established in Yan'an. The United States had been at war with Japan since December 1941, when the Japanese attacked the U.S. naval base at Pearl Harbor in Hawaii. America's entry into

An organized militia unit of the Red Army. The Chinese forces—Communist and Nationalist—both lacked the resources to dislodge the Japanese from the land they occupied. Note, for example, this militia's use of spears as weapons.

World War II brought it into alliance with the Soviet Union (which had been at war with Germany since June 1941) and with Great Britain and France (which had been at war with Germany since 1939). The Americans hoped to persuade the Chinese Communists and the Nationalists to stop fighting each other and to concentrate on fighting the Japanese instead.

The American dream of a united China was not to be realized. Despite the fact that the Americans had appointed him commander in chief of the China-Burma-India (CBI) Theater of War in January 1942 and had given his government millions of dollars in economic and military aid, Chiang was quite content to leave the job of defeating the Japanese to the Americans. For his own part, he simply redoubled his efforts against the Communists. Because the bulk of the American aid to China was funneled through the Nationalists, the Communists saw very little of it. This frustrated some American military leaders in China, especially since it had long been apparent to them that the Communist armies were more effective against the Japanese than Chiang's forces. Prior to 1944, when some of the worst abuses in the Nationalist forces began to be corrected, Nationalist conscripts were, according to American historian Edmund O. Clubb in his book *20th Century China*, often to be seen "roped together to prevent escape." Clubb also states that many of the Nationalist troops "died *even before reaching their assigned units*. Thousands of others, deprived of basic medical care and even their rations by grafting superiors, died of neglect later. As a consequence, the army's generalship was bad, and troop morale was worse. The Nationalist armies sat tight in defensive positions and hoarded their new American weapons for eventual use against [the Communists]. From 1941 to 1944 China's war against Japan was largely in suspense as far as [Chongqing] was concerned. But a strong military

Zhou with Soviet Colonel N. V. Roshchin and U.S. General Joseph Stilwell (1883–1946), in 1943. Stilwell, the commander of U.S. forces in the China-Burma-India Theater of War, tried to get Chiang to fight more forcefully against the Japanese but Chiang resisted, preferring to let others do the fighting.

Zhou with his wife, Deng Yingchao, in 1946. Deng remained an important Communist activist for most of her life.

cordon was set up around the Chinese Communist base in Northwest China."

Chiang's failure to prosecute the war against the Japanese with anything resembling conviction had greatly angered one American soldier in particular—Lieutenant General Joseph W. Stilwell. As U.S. commander for the CBI Theater of War and Chiang's chief of staff, Stilwell had made many sound recommendations for increasing the efficiency of the Nationalist forces. However, since this would have involved making changes in the command structure, Chiang had simply ignored Stilwell. Most of the senior Nationalist officers were Chiang's political cronies, and many of them were, like Chiang, lining their pockets with American money.

The corruption and brutality of the Nationalists often earned them the hatred of the very people they were supposed to be protecting. When the Japanese overran Honan province in 1944, thousands of Chinese civilians rose up in revolt and helped the Japanese massacre the Nationalist troops.

As Governor Chang Chun (left) and U.S. General George C. Marshall (1880–1959) look on, Zhou signs a cease-fire agreement between Nationalist and Communist forces in January 1947. Mediated by Marshall, the negotiations had elicited a warning from Mao to the effect that U.S. backing of Chiang would ultimately prove futile.

Early in 1945, Zhou suggested that a meeting be arranged betwen Mao and Roosevelt, but nothing came of the proposal. Roosevelt died in April, and was succeeded by his vice-president, Harry S. Truman. The war ended in August after the Americans dropped two atomic bombs on Japan.

After the Japanese surrender in August 1945, Zhou accompanied Mao to Chongqing, where a conference was to be held between the Communists and Nationalists. The Nationalists guaranteed Mao's safety, but even so Zhou was careful to taste his food for him, to make sure it had not been poisoned. In the negotiations, observers felt that Zhou was more conciliatory, while Mao took a hard line on future cooperation. It had become increasingly ap-

parent to Mao that the Americans would continue to back Chiang. Soon Mao returned to Yan'an, leaving Zhou to continue hammering out the details of the agreement. Back in Yan'an, Mao's dislike of the pro-Chiang attitudes of the Americans remained intense. During a meeting with Colonel David Barrett, one of the members of the American military mission in Yan'an, Mao lost his temper and declared: "Back [Chiang] as long as you want. But remember one thing. China is *whose* China? It sure as hell is not Chiang Kai-shek's; it belongs to the Chinese people. The day is coming when you will not be able to prop him up any longer."

Even as the two sides attempted to negotiate a compromise and thus establish a reasonable working relationship, both were actively seeking to improve their military positions. During the war, the Communist armies had gained thousands of new supporters, vastly increasing their levels of available manpower. Since it had been a part of their strategy to operate behind the Japanese lines, the Communists had many footholds in areas that Chiang's troops had not entered. However, even though they had expanded their resources, the Communists still had fewer troops and guns than the Nationalists. The advantage enjoyed by Chiang's forces had been considerably enhanced by the Americans, who had cooperated with Chiang by ordering that the Japanese forces in China were to surrender only to Nationalists.

In December 1945 General George C. Marshall, the U.S. chief of staff, flew to China to mediate the dispute. Having persuaded both sides to agree to a cease-fire, Marshall then convinced them that they should work toward establishing a coalition government and that a multiparty consultative conference should be convened to aid this process.

Marshall returned to the United States in March 1946, believing that his efforts had been successful. He arranged for a loan from the United States government to help China rebuild. When Chiang then proceeded to use the loan to finance a Nationalist assault on the Communist troops in Manchuria, Zhou's criticism of U.S. policy toward China became

His is the personality full of mobility, his anger, his earnestness, and his amusement fully set forth in his face. He is one of quick, deft gestures. He will make a photogenic foreign minister.
—JOHN PATON DAVIES
American diplomat,
speaking during World War II,
describing Zhou Enlai

We hope Gen. Marshall will reconcile civil strife in the Northeast in the spirit of the Jan. 10th Truce Agreement. 要求馬歇尔将军本一月十日協定的精神 公平調处东北内战！

Soldiers reading a wall poster following the cease-fire agreement. The truce failed to hold, however, as Chiang continued to try to liquidate his opponents, and the country slipped once again toward civil war.

harsher than ever. "Are you not being a bit mechanically formalistic?" he asked Marshall, who had returned to China on April 18. "Is there not an element of hypocrisy when you know—and everybody knows—that anything you turn over to the Nationalist government goes to the front facing the Communist troops?" The cease-fire failed to hold, and Marshall returned to the United States. He came back to China in October 1946 to arrange another cease-fire, but this time Zhou responded, "There is not enough time; [Chiang] cannot be trusted."

Shortly after Marshall left China for the last time, full-scale civil war broke out in China. At the beginning of the conflict, the Nationalists had the advantage. Their troops outnumbered the Communists by three to one, and in the last half of 1947 they gained several impressive victories and seized vast amounts of territory from the Communists. The Communists evacuated Yan'an and set out on what has been called "the little Long March" to elude the Nationalists. However, their desperate situation was not to last very long. It soon became apparent to the people of China that Chiang's war against the Communists was simply aggravating the appalling problems that had been afflicting the country since the Japanese surrender. Inflation had reached horrendous levels, and many people lost their life savings. The corruption of the Nationalist leaders, combined with the political repression that was a major feature of their rule, only served to increase popular hostility toward them. The Communists soon gained thousands of new recruits, and the Red Army won its first major victories of the civil war in the latter half of 1947.

In 1948 the Communists recaptured Yan'an, took complete control of Manchuria, and moved south toward the Yangzi region. The most crucial battle of the war was fought in central China, on a vast front extending from the Lunghai Railway to the Huai River. The massive, 65-day engagement became known as the Battle of Huai-Hai. The victory that the Communists gained at Huai-Hai established their supremacy in central China. The Nationalists lost approximately 550,000 men, and thousands more defected to the Communist side in the wake of the battle.

By the middle of 1948, it had become obvious that victory was within the Communists' reach. The Chinese Communist party now had 3 million members, and the People's Liberation Army (PLA), as the Red Army had been renamed in 1946, had 2.5 million troops in the field. The PLA advanced rapidly, inflicting staggering losses on the Nationalists, who suffered 1.5 million casualties between September 1948 and January 1949. Chiang assembled the remnants of his loyal forces and fled to the offshore island of Taiwan. There, despite the fact that his conduct during his tenure of power on the Chinese mainland had earned him the hatred of most of the people of China, he would establish a government that he claimed represented all of China.

The Communists are winning the mainland not through combat, but across the negotiation table with Zhou sitting on the other side.
—Guomindang member, speaking during the civil war

A People's Liberation Army unit entering a city in central China in 1949. The tide of the civil war had turned toward the Communists in the last half of 1947. In October 1949, after the army had taken Beijing—Chiang and the Nationalists having fled to Taiwan—Mao proclaimed the People's Republic of China.

In October 1949 Mao and Zhou stood side by side atop the Gate of Heavenly Peace, the entrance to the former imperial palace in Beijing. A vast crowd filled the square below the farm boy and the mandarin's son. Mao's words stirred the crowd: "The Chinese people have stood up . . . nobody will insult us again." Mao then proclaimed the People's Republic of China.

Zhou, at age 51, was appointed premier of the state council and minister of foreign affairs. In the latter capacity he would make his country's influence felt in the arena of international politics. He would show the Western nations that China was now a force to be reckoned with, that Mao had been in earnest when, from atop the Gate of Heavenly Peace, he had said: "The era in which the Chinese people were regarded as uncivilized is now ended."

Starving Hunanese in Kung Ping in the late 1940s.
Chiang's war against the Communists diverted resources
away from the country's much-needed rehabilitation and
greatly increased hostility to his leadership.

4

China Faces the World

When the Communists came to power in 1949, they faced numerous problems on the domestic front. After years of internal disunity, occupation by the Japanese, and civil war, China was in a shambles. The Communist leadership realized that the situation could only be remedied by a fundamental reconstruction program so that people would be assured of the basic necessities of life. To do this, they had to establish a governmental system over the vast nation, unifying it socially and politically. Only after this was accomplished could they hope to implement the radical restructuring of Chinese society that would be required to make the country a communist state.

Zhou, taking the two main governmental posts, was pushed to the limit of his amazing capacity for work. As premier of the state council, he had to design and then supervise an administrative system for the entire country. He looked to the associates and allies he had made in the Communists' struggles of the past 25 years. As foreign minister, he assumed responsibility for establishing China's relations with the other nations of the world.

Zhou set himself a working schedule that he

Oil painting of Zhou by Ho Kung-teh and Kao Hung. The obviously admiring portrait speaks of Zhou's ability—especially during the demanding early years of the People's Republic—to keep in close touch with the Chinese citizenry.

Zhou (second from right) visits the tomb of Vladimir Lenin (1870–1924) in Moscow in January 1950. Because Soviet Premier Joseph Stalin (1879–1953) was said to feel insecure and contemptuous of the sudden rise of a second major communist power, relations between the two countries got off to a bitter start.

73

would follow for most of the rest of his life. In the mornings and afternoons he attended meetings and conferences, at which he was often the featured speaker. In the evenings, he entertained diplomats and other foreign visitors at state dinners. The rest of the night was reserved for reading and writing reports, and also for further discussions with special foreign guests. Zhou continued his practice of sleeping only three hours in the early morning. There were periods when he would go without sleep for days. Visitors always remarked on his relaxed frame of mind and his willingness to devote hours to conversation despite the many other demands upon his time.

In his capacity as chief administrator of the government bureaucracy, Zhou displayed an almost obsessive attention to detail. A Japanese journalist described one of his press conferences thus: "When he is not talking, his eyes never stop moving. If this had not been Zhou Enlai, I would certainly have regarded him as suffering from a nervous breakdown. He would notice the tiniest thing. He made his interpreter pause, for instance, when a waiter quite a distance away caused a little noise while making tea. He himself moved his microphone to the seat of the interpreter next to him. And then, after a while, he stretched out a hand, leaned forward in his chair and with one swing straightened the microphone wire on the floor. It seemed to make him feel uneasy if things were not exactly right."

At the end of 1949, Mao flew to Moscow to appeal for aid. This was the first time he had been out of the country. The treatment to which Mao was subjected in the Soviet Union is poignantly described by American historian Ross Terrill in his book "Stalin at times kept Mao waiting like a message boy. For days at a stretch Stalin had no contact with Mao; and since Stalin did not order anyone to talk to Mao, no Russian dared to go and see him. Mao, feeling isolated, at one point threatened to pack up and return to China." The Chinese Communist victory in the civil war had brought Mao and his colleagues to absolute supremacy over the most populous country in the world. Although it was un-

> *China cannot plunge headlong into democracy such as America, England and other truly democratic countries enjoy. The people of China have been suppressed for so long that they will require generations of political training before they understand the significance and importance of an earnest vote.*
> —ZHOU ENLAI

likely that Beijing would come to supersede Moscow as the focal point of world communism, the balance of power in Asia had shifted in China's favor. As historian Robert Payne explains in his book *The Rise and Fall of Stalin*, Mao was ". . . determined to give to Communist China a special place in the sun . . . [and] represented the kind of Communist that Stalin most abhorred. He owed very little to Stalin and was not prepared to submit to Stalin's will. His armies had conquered China in a single year. Six hundred million people had become the servants of his will. He spoke therefore as an equal, demanded the rights of an equal, and sometimes he would hint that he was even greater than Stalin."

Eventually, Zhou was summoned to Moscow to help speed up the negotiations. Following his arrival on January 20, 1950, the talks continued for several weeks and an agreement was finally reached.

Under the terms of the Sino-Soviet Treaty of Friendship, Alliance, and Mutual Assistance, which

The trial of a landlord in the early 1950s. In the first years of the People's Republic, land redistribution was one of the major domestic imperatives. Peasants were given land taken from former landlords and landowners, some of whom, like the one pictured here, were punished or executed for abuses they had committed.

was signed on February 14, 1950, China received a much-needed credit of $300 million from the Soviet Union. But the rest of the treaty was humiliating for the Chinese. They had to agree to recognize the independent status of Mongolia, which had once been part of the Chinese Empire. The treaty also stipulated that the railways and ports that had been held by Russia as Chinese concessions before 1917 were now to be jointly administered by China and the Soviet Union. Stalin's policies toward China were not much different than those that had been pursued by the Russian emperors, who had generally been both suspicious and contemptuous of their eastern neighbor.

Before the end of 1950, events on China's northeastern border produced a foreign policy crisis that would compel the country to divert its resources from internal reconstruction and to use them to build up its military forces instead. On June 25, 1950, North Korea invaded South Korea, setting the stage for new international tensions.

At the end of World War II, the Korean peninsula

U.S. soldiers marching toward the 38th parallel in Korea in the early 1950s. The direct military confrontation between the United States (on behalf of South Korea) and China (on the side of the North Koreans, who had started the war) did much to strain relations between the two powers.

Cartoon from the *Shanghai News* that appeared in 1951, during the Korean War. The United States, represented by a dollar-sign-covered snake, is receiving simultaneous sword thrusts from the Chinese People's Volunteers at its head and the North Koreans at its tail.

had been divided at the 38th parallel to facilitate the Japanese surrender in that region. The Soviet Union stationed troops in the north, while the United States stationed forces in the south. Although the partitioning of the country had only been intended as a temporary measure, the Soviet Union refused to discuss reunification. Administration of the northern zone was entrusted to the Korean Communist party, and in 1948 the northern zone became the Democratic People's Republic of Korea. In June 1949 North Korean forces began to conduct small-scale raids along the 38th parallel. These raids escalated until the North Koreans launched a full-strength invasion a year later.

The United States' reaction was prompt. President Truman sent troops to South Korea and ordered the Seventh Fleet into the Taiwan Strait to protect Chiang's regime on Taiwan. Zhou denounced the arrival of the Seventh Fleet as an act of "armed aggression on Chinese territory."

The United Nations Security Council condemned the North Korean invasion and authorized "a police action to restore peace." The Soviet Union had earlier walked out of the Security Council, and thus was unable to veto this action against its North Korean ally. (The United Nations, an international organization of the world's states, had been founded in 1945. Its object was to promote peace and international cooperation.)

American General Douglas MacArthur was named commander of the UN expedition. In September 1950 the UN forces effected a surprise amphibious landing behind North Korean lines. It was a brilliant success, and soon the North Koreans had been pushed back to the 38th parallel. The question then arose as to whether the UN forces should pursue the North Korean armies into their own territory, and if so, how far they should advance. Zhou, as foreign minister of China, warned that China "ab-

Chinese soldiers armed with automatic weapons stand at inspection. An estimated 200,000 Chinese soldiers served in Korea and, with the North Korean army, enjoyed great initial success in capturing Seoul, the South Korean capital.

solutely will not tolerate foreign aggression nor will [it] supinely tolerate seeing [its] neighbors savagely invaded." Furthermore, Zhou asked the Indian ambassador to inform the U.S. government that China would enter the war if the UN forces approached the North Korean-Chinese border. The warning was ignored.

On November 26, 1950, the Communist Chinese made good on their threat. An estimated 200,000 Chinese troops came pouring across the border, eventually pushing MacArthur's forces back into South Korea. In January the North Korean and Chinese forces captured Seoul, the South Korean capital.

It was at this point in the conflict that MacArthur asked for permission to attack the Chinese bases in Manchuria. Truman refused, fearing that a direct attack on China might bring the Soviet Union into the conflict. He was determined to avoid a direct confrontation between the two superpowers.

Early in 1951, the UN forces went on the offensive and took back most of South Korea. Cease-fire talks began, and the fighting gradually subsided.

Zhou (center, wearing hat) leads the Chinese delegation into the Palace of Nations in Geneva in April 1954. Zhou had journeyed to Switzerland to take part in negotiations between France and Vietnam's Communists; his efforts helped bring about a settlement and also enhanced his international standing.

The Korean War had long-lasting effects. Although the U.S. had not recognized the Communist government of China, no firm policy had yet been established. Fighting between the two countries created a hostility that would endure for more than 20 years. The United States remained tied to its wartime ally, Chiang Kai-shek, recognizing his regime on Taiwan as the legal government of China. The U.S. lobbied successfully to prevent the People's Republic from taking the Chinese seat in the United Nations.

In 1954 Zhou displayed his considerable talent for international diplomacy at a conference in Geneva, Switzerland. The issue at hand was the war between the Vietnamese Communists (who were led by Ho Chi Minh) and the French colonial government of the country. Zhou used his understanding of both the French and the Vietnamese to bring about a private meeting between representatives of the two sides at his Geneva residence.

At the Geneva Conference, Zhou sought to demonstrate that Communist China was not a mere puppet of the Soviet Union, and that his country would take an independent position on some issues. Zhou cultivated the friendship of British Prime Minister Anthony Eden, hoping that Eden would me-

Zhou dines with North Vietnamese leader Ho Chi Minh (1890–1969) in Beijing during the latter's visit to China in July 1955. Ho, flush from his victory over the French, had turned much of his attention to supporting the Communists seeking to overthrow the South Vietnamese regime.

diate the dispute between the United States and China. However, a chance encounter between Zhou and U.S. Secretary of State John Foster Dulles revealed that there was little chance of the two countries conducting cordial relations. Dulles had already made a statement to the effect that he would not meet privately with Zhou unless "our cars collide in the street."

During a particularly tense period in the negotiations, Zhou was in an anteroom when Dulles entered. Zhou immediately offered his hand. Dulles shook his head and folded his hands behind his back. He left the room, murmuring, "I cannot." Zhou looked around at those who had witnessed the incident, shrugged and lifted his hands. Later he commented that Dulles was "really carrying even reaction to extremes." (In communist terminology, a reactionary is someone who opposes and seeks to undermine communism.) The courtesy that Zhou had shown toward Dulles stood in great contrast to the rudeness and hostility that had characterized the American's response. Zhou's handling of the incident did much to increase his standing with the international diplomatic community.

When the conference went into recess in June 1954, Zhou visited Burma and India, where he tried, without success, to resolve border disputes between those countries and China. He then went on to Vietnam, where he conferred with Ho Chi Minh. Following his return to Geneva, Zhou was largely instrumental in breaking the deadlock at the conference. France agreed to withdraw from Vietnam, and it was arranged that, as a first step toward unification, elections would be held in the northern and southern sections of the country. However, Zhou was unable to persuade the Americans to sign the agreement, though they agreed to abide by its terms.

The elections for which the delegates to the Geneva Conference had called were never to be held. The American government, recognizing that Ho and the Vietnamese Communists would undoubtedly emerge victorious from the elections, decided instead to back a rival regime in southern Vietnam,

Zhou practiced "people's diplomacy." If heads of state were inaccessible, ordinary people could still be reached. From the early 1950s on, China became the site of innumerable conferences of youth and intellectuals who braved government disfavor to practice people-to-people friendships and, inevitably, to meet with Zhou Enlai.

—ED HAMMOND
American historian,
describing Zhou's tactics
as foreign minister
during the 1950s

81

Zhou and Indian Prime Minister Jawaharlal Nehru (1889–1964) ride by motorcade through Beijing during Nehru's October 1954 visit. During Zhou's visit to India the previous June, the two leaders had formulated the principles of peaceful coexistence that serve as the basis for the "nonaligned movement."

and the country remained divided. Assessing his role at the conference, Zhou declared: "We . . . did not have adequate experience in the field of international problems. . . . How can a country which refused to sign the agreement truly be prepared not to impede its implementation? . . . You can criticize us on these grounds. I . . . accept your criticisms."

During his talks in India, Zhou and Jawaharlal Nehru, the prime minister of India, had devised the Five Principles of Peaceful Coexistence, which would form the basis of the foreign policies of those countries that did not wish to align themselves with either the Soviet Union or the United States. The fact that Zhou had cowritten the Five Principles with Nehru, the leader of an important nonaligned nation, meant that even the most right-wing Asian states would be reluctant automatically to brand Communist China a political enemy. The Five Principles were: 1) mutual respect for sovereignty and territorial integrity; 2) mutual nonaggression; 3) noninterference in each other's internal affairs; 4) equality and mutual benefits; 5) peaceful coexistence.

The Five Principles reflected Zhou's shrewd recognition of the fact that many countries felt threatened by the growing enmity between the U.S. and the Soviet Union. Further, China's neighbors feared the rising power of a united Communist China. Zhou sought to reassure them through proclamation of the Five Principles. He said China was willing to have peaceful relations with any country showing the same sincere desire.

Zhou pointed out that China was then in the midst of its first Five Year Plan (a program of national economic reconstruction based upon similar plans that had been originated in the Soviet Union and first implemented there in 1928). He asserted that his country wished to devote its resources to economic development, rather than aggression. "Everyone can see that all our efforts are directed towards the construction of our country, to make it into an industrial, socialist, prosperous, and happy country. We work peacefully and we hope for a peaceful atmosphere and a peaceful world: this fundamental fact determines the peaceful policy of our country as regards foreign policy."

The United States remained unconvinced. It continued to keep Communist China out of the UN. In addition, the United States organized other Asian countries in an alliance called SEATO (Southeast Asia Treaty Organization), which the Chinese regarded as being directed against them.

The United States also sought to reduce China's influence by withholding recognition of its government, and by persuading U.S. allies to do the same. But in 1955, Zhou scored his greatest diplomatic triumph at the Bandung Conference. At the invitation of President Achmed Sukarno of Indonesia, the representatives of 29 African and Asian nations gathered to discuss mutual problems. The conference marked the beginning of an attempt to make those nations to which the Five Principles had primarily been addressed a tangible and internationally effective political bloc.

China was invited to send a delegate to the conference. Zhou suffered an attack of appendicitis two weeks before it was scheduled to begin, and there was doubt about his ability to attend. But he re-

Chiang Kai-shek is opposed to the so-called two Chinas and is also opposed to one China and one independent entity of Taiwan. In the past we have been allied with Chiang Kai-shek, and we became hostile to him, but on this question we have our common point. There can only be one China.
—ZHOU ENLAI

Zhou attends the Afro-Asian conference in Bandung, Indonesia in April 1955, which was the scene of his greatest diplomatic triumph. With one dramatic speech Zhou allayed regional fears of Chinese expansionism, mended fences with many countries, and eased China's general isolation.

cuperated quickly and avoided a further threat when the Taiwanese sabotaged a plane aboard which he had been scheduled to travel.

The first day of the conference was a trying one for Zhou. Some of the representatives of other nations defended SEATO and expressed their fear of Communist China's designs. But when Zhou rose to speak on the second day, he dramatically tore up his prepared speech and addressed the assembly impromptu. Keeping the ideological content of his speech to a minimum, Zhou reminded his audience that all their countries had suffered periods of colonization by Western powers. He also assured them that China would make no attempt to export its revolution to other countries. "The Chinese delegation," declared Zhou, "has come here to seek common ground, not to create divergences. . . . The overwhelming majority of Asian-African countries and peoples have suffered and are still suffering from the calamities of colonialism. If we seek common ground in doing away with these sufferings, it will be easy for us to have mutual understanding and respect."

Chinese Nationalist troops being brought ashore to defend Matsu Island. One of two Guomindang-controlled islands (the other being Quemoy) in the Formosa Strait, Matsu was regarded by the mainland government as its sovereign territory.

The Harbin power plant in northeastern China was part of the government's efforts to increase the country's industrial base. China's economy had remained stagnant through the years of civil war but in the first years of the People's Republic impressive gains were made.

Zhou's diplomatic efforts were immensely successful. More countries recognized the People's Republic of China. China's isolation in trade was eased.

Ironically, the relationship between India and China deteriorated over the next few years. In 1959 the PLA invaded Tibet, a small country bordered by both India and China. (Tibet had been incorporated into China by treaty in 1951). The Chinese invasion came in response to a revolt by the Tibetan clergy and military. According to some reports, about 65,000 anti-Chinese Tibetans were slaughtered. Nehru was extremely upset by the brutality the Chinese had shown in their suppression of the rebellion. India had ancient historic ties with Tibet, and Nehru felt that the Chinese reaction to the revolt had been excessive. The border dispute between the two countries led to an Indian-Chinese war in 1962. Nehru died in 1964, disenchanted with the friendship he had established with Zhou.

Nevertheless, Zhou was widely regarded as a skilled diplomat who won many friends for China

The country has achieved a unity of unprecedented firmness. Bandits, gangsters, superstitious sects and secret societies as well as prostitutes, beggars, gambling houses and narcotic drugs have all been swept away; there is law and order everywhere. The broad mass of the people, united as one and full of vigor, are building their own happy life eagerly, courageously and with boundless energy.
—ZHOU ENLAI
writing in 1959, assessing the progress of the People's Republic of China

Zhou inspects a coal pit at the Kailuan Colliery in northern China in the mid-1950s.

by the benign face he presented to the world. His stress on the common colonial background was particularly successful with the newly independent nations of Africa. During 1963 and 1964 Zhou went on a marathon tour of that continent, receiving a friendly welcome in many countries.

After 1956, China's domestic problems began to demand more of Zhou's attention and energy. The early years of the People's Republic had seen a concentration on land reform and economic development. China was primarily an agrarian country, with over 300 million peasants. In those years, the land was taken from its former landlords and owners and distributed among the peasants. In 1953, the government had initiated a policy of combining the small plots of land into larger, more efficient, collective farms.

The Communist leaders recognized that China would have to increase its industrial base if it was to become a powerful nation. The first Five Year Plan was designed to begin this process. It set realistic production goals, most of which were met. Part of its success was due to Zhou's role in persuading non-Communist professionals and intellectuals to cooperate with the regime.

The role of intellectuals was the subject of much dispute in China because many people viewed them much as they had the mandarins, most of whom had led idle and pampered lives while millions suffered in abject poverty. The Communist leadership recognized, however, that intellectuals would be essential to the success of China's technological and scientific development programs.

In January 1956, Zhou delivered a policy speech on the party's current view of intellectuals. "The overwhelming majority of the intellectuals," he said, "have become government workers in the cause of socialism and are already part of the working class." He added that "the fundamental question now is that the forces of our intelligentsia are insufficient in number, professional skills, and political consciousness to meet the requirements of our rapid socialist construction."

On May 1, 1957, China launched its "Hundred Flowers" campaign, taking its name from a speech in which Mao proclaimed: "Let a hundred flowers bloom and let a hundred schools of thought contend. We Chinese are not afraid of criticism." The official government position was to invite criticism of policies of the government and the party. Some of the leadership, such as Liu Shaoqi, opposed this rash invitation to free speech. But Zhou was among those who persuaded Mao that the criticism would be a constructive step.

The response was far more vehement than any of the leadership had anticipated. People spoke out against the Soviet role in training people for economic development. Others accused the Communists of having failed to deliver on their promises to raise living standards. They condemned the ruthlessness with which the Communists had carried out their land reforms. Criticism was directed toward the party leadership itself, questioning its wisdom and foresight.

Mao and many of his more doctrinaire colleagues quickly declared that the hundred flowers had become "poisonous weeds," and the campaign was sharply curtailed. Those who had encouraged it, including Zhou, fell into disfavor. Zhou lost his post as foreign minister in 1958, and was replaced by Chen Yi, whom he had known since his days in France. But Zhou was still called on to conduct delicate negotiations, and was still sent abroad as the representative of the People's Republic.

Self-criticism is apparent in this cartoon printed in the *People's Daily*. The "Hundred Flowers" campaign launched in 1957 invited criticism of the government and party but was curtailed after it sparked more criticism than expected. Zhou's influence declined as a result of this "failure."

A group of small blast furnaces used during the Great Leap Forward. Though built with great enthusiasm, these "backyard furnaces" produced inferior quality steel and iron and stand as a symbol of a nobly intentioned but badly executed program.

With the decline of Zhou, and his moderating influence, China now set out on a radically ambitious course of development. In 1958, Mao announced the Great Leap Forward—an attempt to industrialize China in one great nationwide program. He emphasized that the success of the Great Leap Forward would depend upon the participation and support of both the workers and the intelligentsia.

Small steel-making furnaces mushroomed all over the country. Thousands of small factories were built to overcome the problems of distribution and transportation of materials. The country's road system was to be extended and upgraded, and its age-old problems of flooding and soil erosion were to be eradicated by the construction of huge dams.

The campaign to create large farm communes also made substantial progress. Private ownership of farmland was declared illegal. The peasants were assigned to communes, which became units of government. The commune owned all personal possessions, and distributed food and clothing according to the needs of its members. All able-bodied adults were required to work 28 days a month.

Although Zhou believed that the targets set by those who had planned the Great Leap Forward were unrealistic, he set a personal example for the program, participating in the construction of a reservoir outside Beijing. Dressed in work clothes, he labored alongside Mao. He "dug up the soil and put it in baskets, sweat dripping from his forehead. When his turn came to flatten the soil, Zhou Enlai not only levelled it but also hardened it with a hoe." Then he joined the line of people passing baskets of earth from hand to hand. Thus did the Communist intellectuals show their difference from the traditional mandarins.

The Great Leap Forward was carried out with much effort and enthusiasm. But these could not make up for poor planning. The iron and steel made in backyard smelters proved to be of poor quality, and factories were idle because the raw materials they needed were not shipped to them. Consequently, many officials falsified production statistics to make it appear that they were meeting their quotas. In addition, bad weather and flooding resulted in reduced agricultural production. Although there are no reliable statistics available, many Western economists believe that the bulk of the Chinese

Zhou made a visit to the Ming Tombs Reservoir in 1958 during the Great Leap Forward, Mao's ambitious plan to speed up the country's modernization. By taking part in physical labor alongside ordinary workers, Zhou and other state leaders highlighted their differences from the estranged mandarin ruling class of pre-revolutionary China.

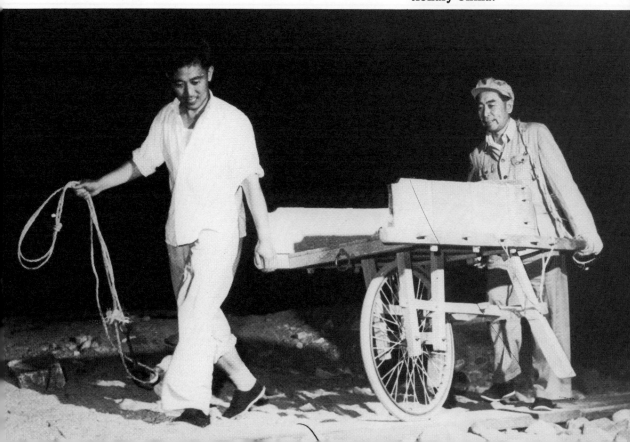

people probably suffered a decline in living standards as a result of the Great Leap Forward.

At a party conference in July 1959, Mao took responsibility for the failure, and faced criticism. "In the past," he said, "the responsibility was on others, such as Enlai. . . . Now I am to blame. . . . Those who were anti-adventurist at the time have now stood firm. An example is Comrade Enlai. He has a lot of energy. Strange that the people who criticized Enlai at that time, this time find themselves in his shoes."

In the next few years, though Mao retained his post as head of the party, his influence declined. Liu Shaoqi, who had been named as Mao's eventual successor, increased his control over the government apparatus.

Zhou now took on the task of China's economic reconstruction. One Chinese professional expressed the opinion, "Zhou will find a way to clean up the mess. He always does." At the party congress of 1962, Zhou paid formal tribute to the Great Leap Forward, and described its failures as due to "serious natural calamities." He then outlined what he

A kitchen scene from one of the farm communes that were established in the 1950s. The government assigned peasants to these agricultural settlements as part of a radical restructuring of Chinese society.

considered more realistic goals for China's development, giving agriculture priority over industry. This summary reversal of previous policy reflected the Communist leadership's awareness of the fact that, in deemphasizing agriculture, the Great Leap Forward had created the danger that China would not be able to feed its people. Economic progress had been set back at least 10 years.

Parallel with the changes in China's domestic situation, the country's foreign policy had also undergone major revision. Friendship with the Soviet Union had always been the bedrock of its foreign relations. In 1952 Zhou succeeded in persuading Stalin to give more aid to China and also to relinquish the privileges that had been allowed the Soviet Union under the terms of the treaty that the two countries had signed in 1950. In 1953 Zhou represented China at Stalin's funeral. The new Soviet leadership gave him a place of honor as the only non-Soviet pallbearer.

Stalin's successor, Nikita Khrushchev, visited the People's Republic to celebrate its national day, thereby according the Chinese Communists a greater role in the international communist movement. But Khrushchev was also concerned with developing better relations with the United States. During his visit to the U.S. in 1959, Khrushchev made statements ridiculing the Great Leap Forward. He refused to give the Chinese the technology that would allow them to build nuclear weapons. The Soviet Union remained neutral in the border war between India and China.

During the late 1950s, there developed a serious ideological rift between China and the Soviet Union. In 1960, the Soviet advisers and technicians in China were suddenly called home. This was the first sign to the outside world that a serious breach had occurred between the two largest communist nations.

The Soviet Union began to put pressure on other communist nations to isolate China. Only Albania, a small, southern European communist nation run by convinced Stalinists, remained a friend of Communist China. When Albania was criticized at the

We advocate peaceful coexistence and peaceful competition between countries having different social systems, and that the people of each country should choose their political and economic systems and their way of life for themselves.
—ZHOU ENLAI
speaking in 1956

Twenty-Second Congress of the Communist party of the Soviet Union (CPSU) in 1961, Zhou, who was representing China at the congress, walked out. He then went to lay a wreath on the grave of Stalin, a gesture of contempt for Khrushchev, who had stunned the delegates to the Twentieth Congress of the CPSU in 1956 by denouncing Stalin and revealing that the Soviet dictator had had millions of Soviet citizens imprisoned or killed on trumped-up charges of conspiracy during the 1930s simply to consolidate his personal supremacy. Khrushchev had informed the CPSU hierarchy that the ruthless methods that Stalin and his colleagues had used in their drive to collectivize Soviet agriculture and to expand the country's industrial base had caused enormous human suffering.

The moderate liberalization of Soviet political life that followed Khrushchev's revelations had shaken the Chinese leaders, who began to refer to Khrushchev and his colleagues as "revisionists"—as

Zhou being greeted in Ghana in January 1964 on the first visit by a Chinese leader to Black Africa. The trip was part of a 72-day, 36,000-mile "safari" through Africa and Asia during which Zhou attempted to establish China as the leader of the Third World.

communists who had abandoned what the Chinese considered the doctrinal purity of the Stalinist method of government. By 1962, the Chinese were openly referring to the Soviet Union as an enemy of the People's Republic.

The Soviet withdrawal of economic and technological aid was a severe loss for China. A series of natural disasters further lowered living standards. With no powerful friends on the international scene, China was isolated and vulnerable. Yet the 1960s would bring one of the most astonishing spectacles in China's long history—the Great Proletarian Cultural Revolution.

Zhou (center) lays a wreath at Stalin's tomb in Moscow's Red Square after walking out on the 22nd Communist Party Congress in October 1961. The gesture was seen as a deliberate affront to the Soviet leader, Nikita Khrushchev (1894–1971), who had denounced his predecessor and also spearheaded efforts to isolate China.

5

Turbulence and Triumph

The years following the failure of the Great Leap Forward saw power in China flow into the hands of Liu Shaoqi. It appears that a rivalry between Liu and Zhou had developed during the Yan'an years. Even so, they appeared to work harmoniously during the lean years from 1959 to 1962.

However, when the economy began to improve, Liu became identified with the right wing of the party. This faction was weary of the attempts to enforce a doctrinaire communist economic system. They were more pragmatic, in that they felt the first goal was to build China's economy and strength—by whatever means proved the most effective. The left-wingers in the party opposed this as an abandonment of socialist principles. They began to call the members of the right wing "capitalist roaders."

Zhou apparently allied himself with the left wing. In December 1964 he gave a speech in which he spoke of new "bourgeois elements" appearing "in society, in Party and government organs." These new bourgeois elements, said Zhou, were "joining hands" with older bourgeois landlords "and other exploiting classes which have been overthrown."

China joined the United States, Soviet Union, Great Britain, and France in the "nuclear club" when it tested an atomic bomb on October 16, 1964.

Zhou delivering a speech during the Cultural Revolution. Zhou championed Mao's campaign to wipe out "bourgeois mentality" by urging students around the country to assist their leader.

During this period, Zhou found himself increasingly at odds with Mao. He suggested to the Ministry of Defense that the time allowed for the training of army recruits be lengthened. However, many senior PLA officers loyal to Defense Minister Lin Biao, who was a protégé of Mao, rejected Zhou's proposals with Mao's approval.

Meanwhile, Liu was consolidating his supremacy in the government and party councils. He managed to place many of his supporters in important posts. Some of his supporters even went so far as to criticize Mao openly. At the beginning of 1966, rumors were circulating that Liu was preparing to depose both Mao and Zhou.

In May 1966 Mao moved to regain his former authority. He announced the beginning of the Great Proletarian Cultural Revolution, which was intended to wipe out the "bourgeois mentality" that Mao believed had arisen during the economic liberalization of the previous four years. People were encouraged to criticize the party, which, according to Mao, had lost its revolutionary spirit. Wall posters, a traditional Chinese form of public expression, called for the overthrow of "rightists." With Mao's approval, students and young workers organized into "Red Guard" units to carry out his revolutionary policies.

In June 1966, during a visit to Romania, Zhou described what was happening in China. "We are determined," he said, "to liquidate completely all the old ideas, all the old culture, all the old manners and habits through which the exploiting classes poisoned the consciousness of the people for thousands of years." Speaking to an audience in Albania, Zhou declared: "In our country, proletarian politics is equivalent to Mao Zedong's Thought. Through his genius and creativeness Comrade Mao has completely inherited and developed Marxism-Leninism. Mao Zedong's Thought represents the Marxism-Leninism of an era in which imperialism is heading toward its extinction and socialism is advancing to victory all over the world. . . ." On his return to China, Zhou visited university campuses and exhorted students "to fan up the socialist wind."

Liu Shaoqi (1898–1974) casting his ballot in the 1959 National People's Congress election in which he was chosen as Mao's successor. Liu's bid for power failed, however, as he lost a factional struggle with Mao, had his Marxist credentials questioned publicly by Zhou, and was a target of suspicion during the Cultural Revolution.

In August Mao himself took the Cultural Revolution to new heights of political fervor, when he encouraged comrades to "bombard the headquarters." Red Guards began to harass government officials and others suspected of "capitalist leanings." One of the victims was Song Qingling, widow of Sun Yat-sen, and Zhou himself moved to protect her.

Perhaps sensing that things were getting out of hand, Zhou persuaded Mao to agree to a number of restrictions on the areas to be subjected to the processes of the Cultural Revolution. Approved by the Chinese leadership on August 8, 1966, the Sixteen Points guaranteed that government operations, economic institutions, and the scientific community would not be harmed by the movement. The Cultural Revolution would be directed only against "rightists" in the party. Zhou seems to have wanted to guarantee that he would be safe in his attempts to keep the country on an even keel. At the same

Zhou and Mao at a mass rally in Beijing during the Cultural Revolution. Zhou acted as a "moderating" influence on Mao when he sensed things might be getting out of hand. As one commentator wrote, those who were worried about any excesses thought that "if Zhou was for it, it _must_ be all right."

北京市革命委员会的成立

Mass rally during the Cultural Revolution. As the movement gained momentum, millions of "Red Guards"—young workers or students given military training to implement the program—staged several marches in Beijing's Tienanmen Square.

> Our [China's] policies are clear-cut ones. We are opposed to the "major powers," to power politics and to domination. We will not become a major power under any circumstances.
>
> —ZHOU ENLAI

time, Mao replaced Liu with Lin Biao as his named successor.

In August a series of enormous Red Guard rallies began in Tienanmen Square, Beijing. Mao, his wife Jiang Qing, Zhou, and Lin were all present to review the scene. More than 11 million Red Guards marched in the rallies. Zhou warned them that they should not interfere with the government or economy for "they have work to do." Despite his reservations concerning the unpredictability and unruliness that were coming increasingly to characterize the political transformation that China was now undergoing, Zhou felt compelled to profess support for the Cultural Revolution. At the National Day celebration, Zhou announced that the Cultural Revolution had "deflated the arrogance of the reactionary bourgeoisie, and is cleaning up all the muck left over by the old society."

The situation began to change rapidly in November, when Lin announced that the Red Guards could criticize the government as well as the party. The Sixteen Points were quickly forgotten, and Red Guards began to drag government officials from their offices. Students, factory workers, and technicians were sent to the countryside to work on farms. Institutions previously protected by the Sixteen Points came under revolutionary assault. Anyone might be accused of being a "capitalist roader" and subjected to beatings, the wrecking of their homes, and even death. The People's Republic began to fall into chaos.

Zhou adopted a position of "shifting with the wind" while doing the best he could to preserve order. As his staff dwindled, he often worked for 30 hours at a stretch, attending to the smallest details of government organization. Finally, however, he himself came under attack. In January 1967 wall posters demanded that Zhou "be burned alive." Zhou presented himself for public criticism at Red Guard rallies, defending himself in abject terms: "I have worked for the Party for many years. I have made contributions and I have also made mistakes.

Chinese youth protest U.S. aggression—meaning support for Taiwan and South Vietnam—during the Cultural Revolution. China's relations with the Soviet Union and with most other countries also suffered during this period of upheaval.

I am striving to keep my complete loyalty to the Party during my late years. This is not passive."

Eventually, Red Guard factions disrupted government at all levels. Local officials were hauled before revolutionary courts to defend their actions. Rival groups of Red Guards fought each other in disputes over which group was following correctly the teachings of "the Great Helmsman," Mao.

Zhou traveled the length and breadth of the country, desperately trying to mediate disputes and restore order. His doctor told him he had heart trouble, and his staff insisted that he cut back on his work load. In April 1967, Red Guards invaded the Foreign Ministry and raided its archives.

During the summer of 1967, a virtual civil war had broken out in Wuhan between rival Red Guard groups, and Zhou went to mediate. When he arrived, his plane had to be rerouted to another airfield, because one faction was waiting to arrest him. In August 1967 the British legation in Beijing was burned to the ground and some of its personnel

Red Guards destroying a signboard in Shanghai because of its capitalist implications. The Cultural Revolution became so extreme in its fervor to purge "capitalist pollution" that the government and party itself were rendered virtually impotent. Even Zhou became a target, with wall posters suggesting that he be "burned alive."

were assaulted by the Red Guards. Zhou rushed to the scene and, visibly angry, ordered the Red Guards to leave.

On August 26 Red Guards besieged Zhou in his office for nearly three days. Neither Lin nor Mao sent reinforcements to dismiss Zhou's attackers. Zhou was left with nothing but his diplomatic skills and energy. With no food or rest, he argued with small groups of Red Guards until they finally withdrew. A few hours later he had a heart attack.

The anarchy created by the Cultural Revolution finally stirred Mao to action. Radicals in Shanghai had set up a commune and urged other cities to do the same. Perhaps remembering the chaos of the warlord-controlled China of the early 1920s, Mao branded this phenomenon, "localism."

Following his recovery from his heart attack, Zhou continued in his endeavors to wind down the Cultural Revolution and pacify the warring factions within the country. In October 1968 he suffered a crushing personal blow when he learned that Sun Weishi, his adopted daughter, had died as a result of the tortures to which she had been subjected by Red Guards. Some commentators have suggested that Zhou was now in such a weak position that he was unable to intervene to save her; others believe that Zhou felt obliged to accord the Cultural Revolution precedence over family ties. It is known, however, that only when the news of Sun's death was made public did Zhou take action. He sent a team of doctors to perform an autopsy, but it turned out that their attentions would not be needed. Sun had been cremated, and those responsible for her murder had disappeared.

Addressing a Red Guard rally at this time, Zhou declared: "We have finally smashed the plot of a handful of top Party persons . . . to restore capitalism." However, Zhou's public optimism was qualified by his private conviction, shared by many others in the Chinese leadership, that the Cultural Revolution had impeded China's development. Ever the survivor, Zhou once more set about trying to put the pieces together.

During the chaos of the Cultural Revolution, one

It is necessary to build socialism with greater, faster, better and more economical results. Is it possible to accomplish this complicated and difficult task? The imperialists and bourgeois elements said that it was impossible. They asserted that 'greater and faster' could not go together with 'better and more economical,' as this would amount to 'keeping a horse running while giving it no feed.' The right opportunists within our ranks echoing them, also said it was impossible. But we firmly replied that it was possible, because we place our reliance first and foremost on the creators of history—the mass of the people.
—ZHOU ENLAI

Zhou with Lin Biao (center; 1908–71) in the late 1960s. Lin, one of the architects of the Cultural Revolution, had been named Mao's successor in 1969 but gradually broke with the chairman and Zhou over the impending visit of U.S. President Richard Nixon.

of Zhou's main concerns was trying to keep an orderly foreign policy. During these years, the United States became deeply involved in the war in Vietnam, on China's border. However, the Chinese Communists had come to consider the Soviet Union an even greater threat to their country's security. In 1968 the Soviet government ordered elements of its armed forces into Czechoslovakia, one of its Eastern European satellite states. The Czech Communists had been trying to liberalize their country's political life and, as far as Moscow was concerned, had deviated from socialism as defined by the Soviet Union. World reaction to the Soviet invasion was highly critical, and the harshest words undoubtedly came from Zhou, who denounced the invasion as "the most bare-faced and most typical specimen of fascist power politics played by the Soviet revisionist clique of renegades and scabs."

The following year, rhetoric escalated into open fighting between China and the Soviet Union in a border dispute. When Soviet Premier Aleksey Kosygin visited China, the conversation he had with Zhou at the airport was so frosty that he immediately returned home.

As relations between China and the Soviet Union continued to deteriorate, Zhou decided to make another attempt to achieve conciliation with the United States. In December 1970 he sent a secret

letter to President Richard Nixon via the government of Pakistan. Zhou stressed that China "has always been willing and has always tried to negotiate by peaceful means . . . a special envoy of President Nixon's will be most welcome in Beijing."

Zhou then made a public overture to the United States by inviting a touring American table-tennis team to visit China. They accepted and the American media covered the event. Zhou told the Americans, "You have opened a new chapter in the relations of the American and Chinese people."

In July 1971 Nixon secretly sent his secretary of state, Henry Kissinger, to Beijing. Kissinger, remembering Dulles's rebuff of Zhou 17 years before, ostentatiously extended his hand to Zhou. The two diplomats had more than 16 hours of talks. Zhou's famous charm made a great impression on Kissinger, who later described Zhou as having "an insinuating ease of manner and a seemingly effortless skill to penetrate to the heart of the matter." However, that Zhou and Kissinger were thus able to establish the beginnings of an understanding could not obscure the fact that relations between their two countries had been characterized by hostility and bitterness since 1949. The United States was still in the midst of a war with China's North Vietnamese allies, and neither side was willing to compromise over the issue of Taiwan. But both wanted to gain an important ally in their opposition to the Soviet Union. Kissinger agreed to investigate the possibility of Nixon making a visit to China.

Some of the members of the Communist Chinese government opposed this new turn in foreign policy. One was Lin Biao, who favored a closer relationship with the Soviet Union. Lin seems to have attempted to stage a coup to overthrow Mao and put himself in power. After an attempted assassination of Mao failed, Lin is said to have tried to escape to the Soviet Union. His plane either crashed or was shot down in Mongolia, and Lin was killed.

In October 1971, Nixon sent Kissinger to China for further talks. This time, Zhou hit on the formula for a statement that would include the opposing views of both sides. Kissinger was impressed by

Men and women should be equal, but there are still old habits that hinder complete equality. We must carry on the struggle. It may take ten or twenty years.

103

Zhou's "extraordinary grasp of the relationship of events. He was a dedicated ideologue, but he used the faith that had sustained him through decades of struggle to discipline a passionate nature into one of the most acute and unsentimental assessments of reality that I have ever encountered."

While Kissinger was returning to the U.S., the United Nations General Assembly voted to admit Communist China to the UN and to expel the Nationalist Chinese government of Taiwan.

When Nixon himself arrived in China in February 1972, Zhou was at the airport to greet him. As they drove to Beijing, Zhou said, "Your handshake came over the vastest ocean in the world—twenty-five years of no communication." The Nixon visit set in motion a new relationship. The American media accompanied Nixon, who toured parts of the country with his wife. The United States seemed to have rediscovered the existence of China.

Nixon met with Mao for "frank and serious discussions." Later, Zhou and Nixon issued the Shanghai Communique, which set forth the differences between the two countries, but also subscribed to the Five Principles of Peaceful Coexistence. The United States agreed eventually to withdraw its recognition of Chiang's government. For Zhou, the fact that the years of hostility between the United States and the People's Republic of China had come to an end was a great personal triumph.

Zhou was not to live to see the official normali-

China's first ambassador to the United Nations, Chiao Kuan-hua, during a debate in the General Assembly. The People's Republic of China was admitted to the United Nations in October 1971, thanks to its official recognition by Third World countries and to Zhou's diplomatic skills.

The changing face of China is seen as a Shanghai street cleaner works under a billboard advertising toothpaste. Such signs of "decadent commercialism" began to proliferate as China's post-Mao leaders reassessed the country's need for economic development.

zation of relations between the two countries. Shortly after Nixon's visit, he was diagnosed as having terminal cancer. However, despite his illness, Zhou continued to work for the future of China, trying to put his homeland on the road to modernization and industrial development. His approach to this enormous task was characterized by his habitual realism. During this period, he informed an American friend that, in his opinion, "China [had] made some progress, but [that it still had] a long, long way to go to approach the material standards of [the United States]." Zhou continued: "It will certainly never happen in our lifetime—nor, in all likelihood, for several centuries."

The China for which Zhou continued to work so hard was still riven by factional infighting. The extreme left of the party was now led by a group of politicians who had become known as the "Gang of

Zhou and U.S. President Richard Nixon (b. 1913) toast each other during Nixon's visit to China in February 1972. Nixon's visit—during which he also met with Mao—ended a quarter century of hostility and mutual suspicion and ushered in an era of peaceful coexistence.

The world could live in peace; if it doesn't, it is because of the misdeeds of the Americans, who are everywhere, and create conflicts everywhere. They are becoming the policemen of the world. What for? Let them go home, and the world will have peace again.
—ZHOU ENLAI
speaking in 1964

Four." The group was headed by Mao's wife, Jiang Qing. Zhou, though not a leader of any faction, supported a return to development and steady economic growth. He sponsored Deng Xiaoping as his deputy and chief of the general staff of the PLA. The aging Mao backed one side and then the other, never letting any faction become powerful enough to gain control. Privately, he was greatly displeased by some of his wife's political activities. The relationship between Mao and Jiang began to deteriorate. In one of his letters to his wife, Mao even went so far as to say: "I do envy the Zhou Enlai marriage."

Zhou made his last public appearance in January 1975, at the Fourth National People's Congress. In a speech that had been approved by Mao, Zhou informed the assembled delegates that China was to implement the "Four Modernizations." These included "modernization of agriculture, industry, national defense, and science and technology before the end of the century, so that our national economy will be advancing in the front ranks of the world."

As Zhou's health declined, he was confined to a hospital bed. To the end, he received foreign visitors and did paperwork in his room. In a rare personal gesture, Mao penned the following poem to his dying comrade:

Loyal parents who sacrificed so much for the
nation never feared the ultimate fate.
Now that the country has become Red, who
will be its guardians?

Zhou with U.S. Secretary of State Henry Kissinger (b. 1923) during the latter's November 1973 trip to China. Kissinger, whose talks with Zhou set the stage for Nixon's historic visit, was a great admirer of Zhou, calling him "one of the two or three most impressive" men he had ever known.

Our mission unfinished, may take a thousand
    years.
The struggle tires us, and our hair is gray.
You and I, old friend, can we just watch our
    efforts being washed away?

With his wife at his side, Zhou Enlai died at 9:57 A.M. on January 8, 1976, in a Beijing hospital, at age 78.

There was neither a guard of honor nor music at Zhou's funeral. Mao was conspicuous by his absence. Silent spectators lined the sidewalks of Beijing as an ambulance bearing his coffin proceeded through the streets. Cars carrying his widow and a few other old comrades followed. The cortege headed into the Western Hills, where the crematorium and cemetery for revolutionary heroes lay.

Later, Zhou's ashes were taken to the Great Hall of the People, where he worked for so much of his life. Deng Xiaoping read a eulogy to a small group of officials. Then the ashes were scattered on the rivers and lakes of China. Shortly thereafter, Deng was ousted from the party and government hierarchy.

In late March and early April, during the Qing Ming festival, in which the dead are remembered, there finally came a spontaneous outpouring of popular grief. People placed wreaths and poems in Zhou's memory on the base of a monument. Though security guards, sent by the left-wing forces of the Gang of Four, soon put a stop to these demonstra-

His gaunt expressive face was dominated by piercing eyes, conveying a mixture of intensity and repose, of wariness and calm self-confidence. He moved gracefully and with dignity, filling a room not by his physical dominance (as did Mao or de Gaulle) but by his air of controlled tension, steely discipline, and self-control, as if he were a coiled spring.
—HENRY KISSINGER
American secretary of state, who visited China in 1971

Discovered only in 1974, these ancient terra cotta statues represent the imperial army of Shi Huangdi (c. 259–210 B.C.), the founder of the Qin dynasty. The 6,000 life-size soldiers and horses are now a major tourist attraction, a fact that attests to China's determination to explore and preserve its rich cultural heritage.

Li Zuopeng (left), Jiang Tengjiao (center), and Huang Yongsheng stand trial on November 25, 1980 on charges that they had conspired to assassinate Mao Zedong and to stage a counter-revolutionary coup d'état.

tions, similar incidents were to occur on the first anniversary of Zhou's death.

Both Mao and Zhu De died later in 1976, which was a year of unusual natural calamities including floods and earthquakes. The Chinese people say that such disasters occur when a dynasty is about to come to an end. Mao, Zhu De, and Zhou were undoubtedly the three men most responsible for the new, Communist order in China, and it came as no surprise to the people that a violent struggle soon erupted over the question of the succession.

Deng Xiaoping emerged as the winner, and speed-

Zhou with People's Liberation Army cadres in 1975. Zhou had been diagnosed in 1972 as having terminal cancer, and the disease kept him bedridden and largely isolated from Chinese political affairs during his final months.

ily deposed the Gang of Four and gained effective control of China. Like his mentor Zhou, however, he refused to accept the top position for himself. Deng found that encouraging the personality cult that grew up around Zhou after his death was an effective way of gaining support for his programs. The Four Modernizations were now the guiding principle behind the policies of the government of China. In 1985, on the 50th anniversary of the Long March meeting that brought Mao the leadership of the Chinese Communist party, the government newspaper accused him of "leftist errors."

The future holds the answer to the question of

Mourners file past Zhou's flag-draped body following his death on January 8, 1976. Though some 10,000 people paid their respects, the ceremonies surrounding Zhou's death were subdued, most likely reflecting intra-party differences over the value of Zhou's accomplishments.

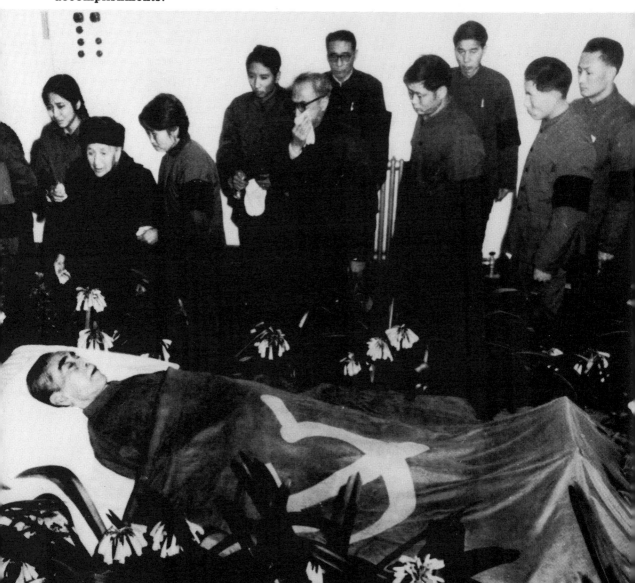

Deng Xiaoping emerged as the leader of post-Mao China. Deng reversed many of Mao's programs, and in 1985 he even allowed statements accusing Mao of having committed "leftist errors" to be published.

Zhou's ultimate importance. If his followers succeed in putting China on a stable course, he will be remembered warmly. For now, his achievement is summed up by Helen Snow, who knew Zhou and Mao in the 1930s: "While Mao Zedong liked to stir up volcanoes in the earth-bound minds of men, Zhou Enlai came along like an engineer to organize the pieces, with the most meticulous attention to detail, superskilled in the art of dealing with the 'Chinese' situation. No ancient mandarin could ever have outfoxed Zhou: Maoism is the art of the impossible; Zhou Enlai-ism is the art of the possible. Mao was a statesman. So was Zhou, but he was also a natural politician . . . a master of teamwork."

Chinese citizens place floral tributes to the late Zhou on the Monument of Martyrs in Beijing's Tienanmen Square. Since his death, Zhou has been recognized as China's most admired 20th-century leader, and his qualities as a statesman and patriot have been invoked in the 1980s promote progressive policies.

Further Reading

Archer, Jules. *Chou En-lai*. New York: E.P. Dutton, 1973.

Clubb, O. Edmund. *20th Century China*. New York: Columbia University Press, 1978.

Hammond, Ed. *Coming of Grace*. Berkeley, California: Lancaster-Miller/Asian Humanities Press, 1980.

Hsu, Kai-yu. *Chou En-lai, China's Gray Eminence*. Garden City, New York: Doubleday & Co., Inc., 1969.

Kissinger, Henry, *White House Years*. Boston, Massachusetts: Little Brown & Co., 1979.

Salisbury, Harrison E. *China: 100 Years of Revolution*. New York: Holt, Rinehart & Winston, 1983.

Snow, Edgar. *Red Star Over China*. New York: Grove Press, Inc., 1968.

Snow, Helen Foster. *My China Years*. New York: William Morrow & Co., 1984.

Wilson, Dick. *Zhou Enlai*. New York: Viking Press, Inc., 1984.

Chronology

March 5, 1898	Born Zhou Enlai in Huaian
Feb. 12, 1912	Last Manchu emperor abdicates
1913–17	Zhou attends Nankai Middle School in Tianjin
Sept. 6, 1919	Founds the Awakening Society, an attempt to unite the disparate protest groups in the May Fourth Movement
1920–24	Lives in Europe where he joins the Chinese Communist party
1924–27	As member of both Nationalist and Communist parties, participates in military campaigns against regional warlords
April 12, 1927	Shanghai uprising led by Zhou thwarted when Nationalist troops turn against the Communists
1928–31	Zhou lives in Shanghai under false identity after Communist party forced to operate underground
1931	Communists move headquarters to Jiangxi province Zhou appointed political commissar of the Red Army
Oct. 16, 1934	Communist forces, after several decisive losses to the Nationalists, withdraw from their bases and begin 6,000-mile retreat known as the Long March
1935	Communists encamped in caves in the Shaanxi hills
Dec. 1936	Capture of Chiang Kai-shek in Xi'an by the Young Marshal's troops leads to the resurrection of the Communist-Nationalist United Front
1937–45	China fights Japan in World War II
1946	Full-scale civil war breaks out after attempt by U.S. General George C. Marshall to negotiate truce fails
Oct. 1949	The People's Republic of China founded Zhou named premier and minister of foreign affairs
Feb. 14, 1950	Signs Sino-Soviet Treaty of Friendship, Alliance and Mutual Assistance
1950–53	Korean War
May 1, 1957	China launches "Hundred Flowers" campaign, inviting open criticism of government programs and party positions
1958–59	China implements the Great Leap Forward, a massive industrialization program
1961	Zhou walks out of Twenty-Second Congress of the Communist Party of the Soviet Union
1966–76	Great Proletarian Cultural Revolution
1971	Zhou twice hosts Henry Kissinger, the U.S. secretary of state
Feb. 1972	U.S. President Richard Nixon visits China
Jan. 8, 1976	Zhou dies, aged 78, in Beijing, of cancer

Index

Dorothy and Thomas Hoobler live and work in New York City. They have written many books on history for young people, including *U.S.-China Relations Since World War II*, and *Joseph Stalin* in the Chelsea House series WORLD LEADERS   PAST & PRESENT.

Arthur M. Schlesinger, jr., taught history at Harvard for many years and is currently Albert Schweitzer Professor of the Humanities at City University of New York. He is the author of numerous highly praised works in American history and has twice been awarded the Pulitzer Prize. He served in the White House as special assistant to Presidents Kennedy and Johnson.